Cambridge Elements

Elements in Religion and Monotheism
edited by
Paul K. Moser
Loyola University Chicago
Chad Meister
*Affiliate Scholar, Ansari Institute for Global Engagement with Religion,
University of Notre Dame*

MONOTHEISM
AND SOCIAL JUSTICE

Robert Karl Gnuse
Loyola University New Orleans

CAMBRIDGE
UNIVERSITY PRESS

CAMBRIDGE
UNIVERSITY PRESS

Shaftesbury Road, Cambridge CB2 8EA, United Kingdom

One Liberty Plaza, 20th Floor, New York, NY 10006, USA

477 Williamstown Road, Port Melbourne, VIC 3207, Australia

314–321, 3rd Floor, Plot 3, Splendor Forum, Jasola District Centre, New Delhi – 110025, India

103 Penang Road, #05–06/07, Visioncrest Commercial, Singapore 238467

Cambridge University Press is part of Cambridge University Press & Assessment, a department of the University of Cambridge.

We share the University's mission to contribute to society through the pursuit of education, learning and research at the highest international levels of excellence.

www.cambridge.org
Information on this title: www.cambridge.org/9781009223317

DOI: 10.1017/9781009223300

First published 2023

A catalogue record for this publication is available from the British Library.

ISBN 978-1-009-22331-7 Paperback
ISSN 2631-3014 (online)
ISSN 2631-3006 (print)

Monotheism and Social Justice

Elements in Religion and Monotheism

DOI: 10.1017/9781009223300
First published online: June 2023

Robert Karl Gnuse
Loyola University New Orleans

Author for correspondence: Robert Karl Gnuse, rkgnuse@loyno.edu

Abstract: The rise of monotheistic religious faith in ancient Israel and post-exilic Judaism inspired the imperative for social justice on behalf of the poor and the oppressed. Though some authors have maintained that monotheism inspires tyranny, this author maintains that real monotheistic faith affirms justice and human equality. This can be evidenced by a consideration of the Old Testament prophets and Law. Especially with the Law we may observe a progression in the attempt to provide increasing rights for the poor and the oppressed.

Keywords: monotheism, social justice, Old Testament prophets, Old Testament Law, Babylonian Exile

ISBNs: 9781009223317 (PB), 9781009223300 (OC)
ISSNs: 2631-3014 (online), 2631-3006 (print)

Contents

Introduction

Our modern world faces many challenges in the areas of environmental protection, global warming, poor universal human health, adequate food for all people, clean water resources, human rights, legal justice, equality for all people, and extensive human poverty, the last of which may be central to those other issues (Bills, 2020: 2). In regard to those last issues, a discussion of religion and human rights is valuable, and in particular, a discussion of how religious monotheism provides significant rhetorical and moral support to social justice. Monotheism is the inherent assumption among three great religions of our age, Judaism, Christianity, and Islam, which together claim the allegiance of the vast majority of people in our world. Their beliefs shape the world's culture to a monumental extent both historically and culturally. To the best of our understanding monotheism appears to have emerged among Israelites and Jews in the first millennium BCE who bequeathed this persuasion to the later religions of Christianity and Judaism. The understanding of how monotheism emerged among Zoroastrians is uncertain among scholars and a discussion that goes beyond the scope of this essay.

Modern scholars recognize that monotheism, perhaps intolerant of belief in the existence of other gods, only emerged among some of Jewish people in the Babylonian Exile of the sixth century BCE, or even later in the post-exilic period. When the Jewish intelligentsia in exile were surrounded by people worshipping other deities, Jews had to make the decision to worship only one god or conform to the religious beliefs of their neighbors. Pre-exilic prophets and reform movements of kings Hezekiah and Josiah may have provided the early stages necessary for monotheistic commitment without being monotheistic per se. Polytheism was regnant among Israelites until the exile in 586 BCE as is now evidenced by both archaeological discoveries and a fresh look at texts in the Bible that testify to the diversity of religious belief in Israel and Judah. New scholarly paradigms arose as scholars looked at all this information in a new way, especially the biblical texts.

Monotheism may result from many social-historical experiences of the human condition, including political and religious conflicts, challenges and upheavals for the people. Perhaps, events leading up to the emergence of monotheism may have included the Phoenician Baalism in the ninth century BCE that aroused the response of Elijah and Elisha, economic conditions and oppression in both Israel and Judah of the eighth century BCE which inspired classical prophets, the threat of Assyria to Judah in the late eighth century BCE that caused Hezekiah's reforms, the collapse of Assyria in the late seventh century BCE which set in motion the reforms of Josiah, and the destruction of

Jerusalem in 586 BCE and subsequent exile in Babylon. Religious change often accompanies social upheaval. Traumatic experiences assure the ultimate success for monotheism. Various scholars have discussed all of these events as possible catalysts in the process of emerging monotheism, although some scholars dismiss some or all of these events as literary creations in the biblical text, saying the monotheism arose completely in the exile or thereafter.

Among the many scholars who have contributed to this new paradigm from 1980 to 2005 the following authors are significant: Bernard Lang (Lang, 1983), Mark Smith (Smith, 1990, 2001), Rainer Albertz (Albertz, 1994a: 77–96, 1994b), and other essays in volumes edited by Othmar Keel (Keel, 1980), Walter Dietrich and Martin Klopfenstein (Dietrich and Klopfenstein, 1994), and Diana Edelman (Edelman, 1996).

Giovanni Garbini (Garbini, 1988), Herbert Niehr (Niehr, 1990), and Philip Davies (Davies, 1992) believe monotheism did not arise until the Maccabean era. I have attempted to summarize the contributions of these authors (Gnuse, 1997: 62–188, 1999: 315–36).

Erich Zenger (Zenger, 2003: 9–52) and André Lemaire (Lemaire, 2007: 99–116) both provide more recent and succinct discussions of emerging monotheism.

Significant variations to the new paradigms have recently been proposed. James Anderson dismisses efforts of Hezekiah and Josiah, maintaining that the Omrides in the mid-ninth century BCE introduced Yahweh as the national god of Samaria, thus paving the way for post-exilic monotheism (Anderson, 2015: 99–121).Or again, a discussion has arisen over concerning the origin of Yahweh. The old scholarly paradigm, the "Midianite Hypothesis," that Yahweh was brought into the land from the south, or southeast, perhaps Edom, that the name was first revealed to Moses while he lived with Jethro the Midianite, and that this deity was elevated to national status by David, has been questioned. André Lemaire (Lemaire, 2007: 19–28, 35–42) and Erich Zenger (Zenger, 2003: 17–20) most recently have summarized that model in clear fashion. But Henrik Pfeiffer and others have proposed that Yahweh was a storm god who originated within the land of Palestine or came down from Syria and was elevated to become a national deity by the Omrides in Samaria in the ninth century BCE (Pfeiffer, 2015, 2017: 115–44). Thus, our scholarly paradigms have been in flux for two generations.

If we attempt to arrive at a working model for our discussion, we might suggest that spokespersons for the Yahwistic religion prior to the sixth-century BCE exile called for the exclusive worship of Yahweh without necessarily being advocates of a monotheism that denied the existence of other gods. This has been called monolatry by some scholars in the past, which is a practical monotheism that treats Yahweh as though he were the only god in the divine realm worthy of worship and veneration without denying the existence of other gods. It has also been called henotheism, a religiosity that elevates one deity to supremacy over the other gods, "a heavenly host," that is regarded with respect as a group of divine beings that, however, did not merit the worship of individual gods (though some might engage in such devotion for particular needs). Much scholarly ink has been spilled over these two terms, so a developed discussion would be beyond the scope of this work. I shall prefer to speak of pre-exilic Israelite and Judahite advocates for Yahweh as proclaiming a message of "exclusive" worship of Yahweh, leaving aside the issue of the veneration of those other divine beings who either served or opposed Yahweh.

Stricter monotheism emerged during the Babylonian Exile of the sixth century or in the post-exilic era, for that was an age in which the leaders of Judahite society, including the intelligentsia, found themselves as prisoners in a foreign land. The crisis of being surrounded by religionists of another faith demanding that the Judahites conform to their culture and religious beliefs forced the Judahites to make a decision. Would they assimilate to Babylonian culture or maintain their identity? Those who chose the latter option then had to make a religious decision to deny the existence of the gods of their captors and affirm the sole existence of the deity of their old homeland, Yahweh. In so doing, they had to develop an intolerant form of monotheistic faith and become Jews.

It takes a crisis for a breakthrough to monotheism to occur, for monotheism will not naturally develop out of polytheism. That would be unnatural. The human mind perceives the divine all around in the world, so envisioning the presence of many gods is natural. Human needs for crop fertility, healing, and other deep existential needs also demand a natural polytheistic view of reality. Monotheism emerges only with a special crisis situation, such as exile in a foreign land with pressure of foreign religionists laid upon you.

For this reason, I shall use the term "monotheism" to describe the religiosity of that later era. This does not come without problems. It is most likely that a consistent monotheism, or an intolerant monotheism that denies the existence of the other gods, was a world view of only a few Jewish intelligentsia, who included those who generated our biblical texts. The majority of the people that we might be tempted to call monotheistic in this era were still polytheistic deep in their hearts, for the old gods are hard to surrender, especially a mother goddess who is most popular among women and a healing god or goddess.

Gradually monotheism gained the hearts of the people, so that perhaps by the second-century Maccabean era, perhaps the vast majority of Jews could be counted as monotheists. Although one might challenge this on the basis of references to divine beings in some of the Jewish literature, and the natural proclivity of common folk to hold on to such divine numina for reasons of personal health, crop fertility, and other deep personal needs. Perhaps, the vast majority of Jews became monotheists in the Rabbinic era, or perhaps the modern era. We cannot look into the minds of people in their moments of need to truly access this process. Certainly the beliefs of monotheism developed unevenly among the people for many centuries, and the point in time when the ultimate victory of monotheism among the vast majority of people would probably surprise us for how late it occurred.

In the recent generation many scholars have suggested that the use of the word "monotheism" might be inappropriate as a moniker to describe Jewish religious identity even in the post-exilic era due to the presence of so many divine beings in the popular piety, and the inherent exclusivity implicit in the word, which did not describe the beliefs of a majority of the people. I recognize that cogency of their critique, but nonetheless, I will use the word as a practical description for the religious beliefs of that age. The word can be used to characterize the literature produced by the intelligentsia which became sacred text, even if those intelligentsia constituted a minority of the populace and their views were but a "minority report," designed to persuade the rest of their co-religionists of the truth of monotheistic faith. These intelligentsia, after all, produced the sources that we have and the literature that has inspired millions of people for thousands of years. This is the literature that I believe has inspired and undergirded the call for social justice among so many political and social reformers in the modern era.

Thus, for practical purposes in this text, I shall refer to pre-exilic spokes-persons and their texts as advocates for the "exclusive" worship of Yahweh, and I shall reserve the use of the word "monotheism" for those who articulated religious rhetoric for Jews during and especially after the sixth-century BCE exile. I also recognize that the sixth-century BCE exile for Jews lasted many centuries after the sixth century because the majority of Jews never returned to Palestine from Babylon. Perhaps the "Babylonian Exile" lasted until 1947 when so many Jews did return from Iraq to the newly forming state of Israel. Furthermore, I also recognize that many Jews in exile were in Egypt and other places throughout the ancient world. For this reason, "monotheism" emerged slowly and irregularly among Jewish folk after 500 BCE, and truly was the belief system of a minority of the people. This may best be demonstrated by our discovery of the polytheistic inclinations of Jews in Egypt, at Elephantine, in the fifth century BCE, a rather late time for it to exist according to some of our paradigms. But for practical purposes in this discussion we shall use the term "monotheism" to describe the faith of Jews in the post-exilic period. Many of the prophetic oracles and legal texts connected to the cry for social justice, which we shall discuss later in this volume, arose in the time when the call for "exclusive worship" of Yahweh arose and before the emergence of what we call "monotheism."

The call of exclusive worship of one God and ultimately monotheistic rhetoric were made in the Israelite and Jewish environment in the middle and late first millennium BCE. Religious thought in the ancient Near East provided raw materials for sensitive religious thinkers in Israel, both in the pre-exilic era and especially during the exile. Israelites did not evolve up from a simple set of beliefs to monotheism; rather, they inherited a complex set of ideas, which they amalgamated them into their own distinctive worldview in what can be described as a reconstruction, reconstrual, or reconfiguration of the thought of predecessor cultures (Hayes, 1971: 136; Porter, 1979: 131; Brueggemann, 1985: 28–46; Miller, 1985: 207; Frick, 1985: 193–4). William Dever has cleverly characterized this Israelite intellectual achievement as a "mix" or "configuration" of the "traits" of those predecessor cultures (Dever, 2000: 67). This was an evolutionary development, which had gone on in the ancient world for many years, but a significant leap occurred with the fruition of Israelite thought in the Babylonian Exile.

Literary-artistic breakthroughs were being made at this time in a cultural arena from India to the Balkans (Gnuse, 1997: 210–18). Karl Jaspers used the term "Axial Age" to describe this age of revolutionary development (800 BCE to 400 BCE) (Jaspers, 1953), and subsequent authors have used the concept (and sometimes called it the "Axis Age") (Cobb, 1967: 52–106; Tremmel, 1984: 125–45; and essays in Eisenstadt, 1986). Whether this is an apt historical designation has been questioned by a significant number of scholars, but I believe this does describe the intellectual development of the first millennium BCE. This was an age of great development in the high religions (Upanishadic Hinduism, the Code of Manu, Buddhism with Siddharta, Jainism with Mahavira, Confucianism, Taoism, Achaemenid Zoroastrianism, and Second Temple period Judaism), the emergence of significant thinkers in the Greek world (Homer and Hesiod; the pre-Socratic philosophers; Socrates; historians such as Hellenicus, Hecateus, Herodotus, Thucydides, and others; tragedians, such as Aeschylus, Euripides, Aristophanes, and others; scientists such as Hippocrates, Pythagoras, and others), as well as nameless individuals in other societies, who contributed greatly to the development of world culture. The emergence of empires in the first millennium BCE facilitated the spread of more extensive trade, which encouraged the spread of ideas that inspired advanced intellectual reflection. This was the era in which exclusive devotion to Yahweh and ultimately monotheism arose.

1 Tyranny or Justice? The Debate

The Nature of Monotheism

Does monotheism engender social justice? In order to justify writing this volume with such a title, we must provide examples of the imperative to social justice found in a monotheistic religion. We must also answer how the dynamics of a monotheistic faith can encourage its devotees to seek social justice. We shall address those two issues in later sections. But first we must speak about the great debate concerning whether monotheism inherently encourages equality, human dignity, and justice, or whether it more naturally encourages tyranny.

Frequently I have heard it said in oral presentations, convention papers, and written publications that oppression of women, centuries-long existence of slavery, justification for war, pollution of our environment, and other woes of human society result from teachings in the Bible as well as the basic beliefs of monotheistic faiths. In response I have written several works to demonstrate that the biblical tradition, in particular, speaks of liberation, human freedom, egalitarianism, human dignity and social reform (Gnuse, 1985, 1997: 274–97, 2000: 141–57, 2007: 78–95, 2011). More recently, I have argued that the Bible, if properly read, does not permit the unbridled pollution and destruction of our environment (Gnuse, 2021a: 64–71, 2021b: 168–74, 2021c: 4–14). I have also argued that the Bible does not really condemn same sex relations between two people who are adult, free, and truly in love (Gnuse, 2015a: 68–87, 2015b: 117–60, 2021d: 33–41). I have frequently said that if anyone uses the biblical text to oppress anyone, whether it be on the basis of wealth, sex, race, or sexual identity, they are brutally misusing the Bible. The Bible is a book of liberation. If you do not believe that it is divinely inspired, at least recognize that it was created by intellectuals well ahead of their time and culture (and sometime still ahead of where we are at today).

Critics who attribute the source of such woes to the Bible can indeed point to the message of fundamentalist preachers who have used the Bible in the modern age to subordinate women, attack homosexuality, attack the theory of evolution, affirm the inferiority of African Americans, defend the notion of a just war as the solution to most international crises, and in the early nineteenth century such preachers also justified the existence of slavery. But this is a misuse of the Bible. A deeper understanding of the biblical text reveals that it speaks of equality and respect for the poor, the oppressed, slaves, women, and others so often crushed by the social and economic forces in our world. Sadly too many people listen to the messages of the evangelical preachers and believe them, or want to believe them.

Critical intelligentsia who so quickly condemn monotheism and the biblical message do not understand that the biblical texts were generated in the first millennium BCE (Old Testament) and the first century CE (New Testament), products of a repressive and patriarchal age. The biblical stories reflect the everyday life and values of that era. To know the real values of the biblical authors, we must view the biblical laws that sought to reform society, the prophetic oracles that attacked oppressive religious and social practices, and the writings of the New Testament. Compare the biblical writings to the values of their culture, which they sought to uplift, but do not compare them unfairly to our modern values. We live two millennia years later, and much of our egalitarian beliefs, which place us beyond the values of the biblical authors, were inspired to develop by those very same biblical authors.

We must also be sensitive to the development within the biblical tradition itself, both in terms of emerging monotheism and evolving social practices. There is an evolutionary process on several issues within the biblical tradition which demonstrates how biblical authors increasingly sought to redress the wrongs of society and affirm the exclusive worship of one god. The Bible is not a static and timeless book; rather, it inspires an evolutionary trajectory that begins with it and moves forward into the future. When a biblical passage is critical of slavery in the first millennium BCE without necessarily calling for abolition, that message should really translate into abolitionism in the modern era, as it did in nineteenth-century America. When an early biblical text subordinates the other gods to a retinue of servants underneath Yahweh, it is taking a major step toward abolishing those gods altogether in later years.

A good example is how biblical texts inspired political thinkers in America in the eighteenth century. From 1760 to 1805 American political authors drew 34 percent of their citations from the Bible compared to 22 percent drawn from Enlightenment thinkers, 18 percent from Whig authors, 11 percent from common law, and 9 percent from classical sources (Lutz, 1984: 189–97, especially 192; Gnuse, 2011: 6–8).

Democracy did not exist in the first millennium BCE, but biblical ideas ultimately resulted in the emergence of democratic thought among the deists who were our founding fathers. The Bible invites us to move beyond where the biblical authors were intellectually, especially on matters of justice.

A religious and intellectual revolution began over 2,000 years ago, and we live in the midst of that on-going and not yet finished revolution. It was a revolution to revere one god exclusively and to create a just social and economic society. Perhaps because we do not readily sense the great patterns of history in our lives, we do not appreciate that we still live in that continuing revolution that is changing the religious, intellectual, and social assumptions of human culture. The revolution is the emergence of monotheistic religious beliefs with their concomitant intellectual and social values. It may sound strange to call something a revolution that has lasted for 2,000 years, but it is a short period of time compared to the vast eons of time involved in human evolution. Emergence of monotheism is but a fraction of civilized human history, which began when we settled in villages around 9500 BCE in the Near East.

The emergence of the exclusive worship of one god and a call for justice in the biblical testimony was both revolutionary, but also evolutionary, as we may observe the stages of development within the biblical tradition, and the unfolding of its implications in terms of justice is still emerging in our own. Thus, the Old Testament was critical of the oppressive aspects of slavery, the New Testament sought to abolish the distinction between slave and free in the Christian community, modern liberal Christianity gave rise to the modern abolitionist movement, and today we still seek to abolish forms of wage and sex slavery throughout our world. For years I have used the expression "emergent monotheism" to describe the process of unfolding the beliefs and social values of monotheism.

Certain assumptions and ideas in the biblical text could not be fully developed in that initial biblical age, but only when human culture was ready for their fuller actualization. Emergent monotheism creates a trajectory, an on-going developmental process of religious beliefs and social imperatives, which would bring greater equality and respect for all people, the abolition of slavery, concern for the poor, the affirmation of human rights for everyone, and various social reform movements. It took a long time for the monotheistic beliefs of Judaism and Christianity to bring about these advances in modern society, but ideas and practices cannot be implemented immediately. Such values reside in the belief system latently, and they await the time in human history when they can become manifest. Recognition of this process should lead us to continue to advance the monotheistic "evolution" in our own age, as we advocate social justice.

Response to the Critics of Monotheism

Some contemporary authors maintain that monotheism does not bring human equality and justice to society, but rather it is the source of repression and even violence. They decry monotheism for undergirding tyrannical governments, justifying the institution of slavery, and legitimating the radical subordination of women.

Regina Schwartz declares that monotheism engenders violence and oppression (Schwartz, 1997). I have responded to her arguments in the past in greater detail (Gnuse, 2007: 78–95). She declares that belief in one God implies that

God favors a specific group of people, gives them a unique identity, and inspires them to exclude or attack others. In both the Old Testament and Christianity, the notion of covenant leads the religious community to create an identity and scapegoat others outside that community. Though the Bible mandates love of the neighbor, when that neighbor challenges our identity, then that "neighbor" must be opposed. Initially, monotheism unifies people peacefully to share scarce resources, such as land and wealth, but when monotheism is combined with the "particularism" of a covenant relationship, it becomes aggressive. The gods of other peoples are idols, and if those people worship idols they become abominations (Schwartz, 1997: 33). Identity is connected to land, which reinforces the desire to possess, defend, and conquer. Divinely promised land is bequeathed from God and its possession is maintained by obedience to that God, which involves military aggressiveness. After the gradual return of Jews from the sixth-century BCE exile in Babylon, obedience to God and emphasis upon purity, led the Jews to be hostile toward foreigners. They told the story of how the earlier exodus freed slaves, who then conquered Palestine and killed Canaanites. Though monotheism declares that all people worship the same God, theoretically creating a toleration of others, too often it generates imperialism that seeks to conquer and others.

Schwartz does acknowledge that there is an alternative. Ethical values are affected by a scarcity of food, water, land, and other precious resources, which must be shared by people for self-survival. Though monotheism proclaims that the resources are to be had by the chosen few, the biblical text must be used so that an "ethic of scarcity" may be replaced by an "ethic of plenitude" in which all humanity shares in the world's resources. I believe the biblical text indeed proclaims such an ethic, and monotheistic universalism may generate toleration rather than imperialism. Schwartz admits exclusive monotheism does not necessarily produce a violence (Schwartz, 1997: 31).

I believe that the problem is not with monotheism, but with how the Bible is interpreted. Schwartz really attacks the misuse of those accounts by modern believers who use them to justify some form of continued subordination of other people.

Modern Jews and Christians view the narratives of the Old Testament through later texts: Jews use the Talmud, and Christians use the New Testament as the hermeneutical key by which to understand those older biblical texts. Thus, some nationalistic and violent expressions in the older texts (holy war) have been transcended by later Christianity and Judaism. Earlier and cruder values in the biblical text are overturned by later revelation and human religious insight in that very same biblical text. Monotheism and social justice emerge over the years.

Robert Goldenberg responds to scholars who see an inherent intolerance in monotheistic movements (Goldenberg, 1988: 1–108). Goldenberg refers to Johannes de Moor's observations that the fourteenth-century BCE monotheistic religious reform of Pharaoh Akhenaten in Egypt created an oppressive religion and the views of Elias Bickermann that post-exilic Judaism and the Hebrew Bible undergirded monotheistic intolerance (de Moor, 1990: 44; Bickermann, 1967: 91). Goldenberg accepts that pre-exilic Israelites were largely polytheists and only after the exile were Jews truly monotheistic. He views the biblical text from the perspective of the exilic and post-exilic authors who gave the biblical text its final form. Jews had mixed views about other religionists from the biblical era through the rabbinic period. Some Jews condemned the religions of others, while others believed that the peoples of the world worshipped their god indirectly (especially in the Hellenistic and Roman eras). Some felt that Gentiles should be converted; while others believed they should be left alone, as long as they did not convert Jews. Thus, Judaism was not an intolerant religion; Jews also sought alternatives to the intolerance of some of their co-religionists. Goldberg addresses the question of monotheistic tyranny, for in demonstrating the diversity of opinion found in various biblical and extra-biblical texts on this one issue, he prevents us from seeing monotheistic Judaism as monolithic and intolerant to other religions.

Jeremiah Cataldo provides an evaluation from a very different perspective, which is somewhat neutral yet ultimately critical in its assessment of monotheism. He maintains that monotheism originated in a conflict for land and authority between a religious body and a larger social entity. His primary test case is post-exilic Judah under the religious rule of the priests when the province of Yehud is also part of the greater Persian Empire. Monotheism was used as a tool to organize the province of Yehud under Priestly leadership, as well as the individual leadership of Ezra and Nehemiah. It arose to define the community of Yehud and the people in it, and to exclude others from that particular religious and social definition provided by the texts and enforced by the newly created leadership. The exclusion of others provided not only identity, but strong authority for those leaders. Thus, monotheism does not evolve out of polytheism, says Cataldo, nor is it a breakthrough (as I have said in earlier writings, which he critiques). Only in later years, he believes, when no longer used for purposes of political and social community definition, will monotheism become free to become ideational and subsequently to become a religion (Cataldo, 2012). His assessment is detailed and brilliant, but he overlooks some factors. The call for the exclusive worship of Yahweh is found among pre-exilic prophets, unless you claim that the prophetic corpus is completely a post-exilic fiction. Likewise, reforming laws in the pre-exilic era also appear to be connected to the exclusive worship of Yahweh. Prior to the creation of Yehud in the fifth century BCE, there were to be found among the Israelites and Jews significant seeds that would germinate into the more exclusive monotheism of the post -exilic period. It is the exile in Babylon that provided the breakthrough, which Cataldo denies, when Jews found themselves surrounded by other religionists worshipping Marduk and other gods. For then they had to decide firmly that there is no god in the heavens other than Yahweh, or else they would lose their identity and simply become Babylonians. Or least those Jews who survived the exile were the ones who made this decision. There indeed was an ideational and social origin to monotheism prior to its political use in the fifth century BCE. By Cataldo's thought there was no evolution, no breakthrough, and apparently monotheism arose politically in the fifth century. But ideas moving in a monotheistic direction existed for centuries prior, and the use of monotheism to politically and socially undergird a post-exilic province in the Persian Empire is but a stage in its development. Cataldo overlooks that monotheism might first have provided an ideational or religious force for creating identity before it became a political force for creating identity in the fifth century BCE. In general, he overemphasizes the political dimension far too much.

Imperial or Liberating Monotheism?

Genghis Khan reputedly said, "In heaven there is no-one but the one God alone; on earth no-one but the one ruler Genghis Khan"(Moltmann, 1985: 51). One could also easily attribute this notion to Constantine who believed in one faith, one God, one ruler (Kirsch, 2004: 171–2). Several authors see this as a summary of monotheism. The one majestic God in the divine realm legitimates the powerful autocrat on earth. As people should be devoted to that one God, so also their political allegiance should be to the one ruler who represents that God. The ruler will be inclined to convert others to that God and his rule. A monotheistic state will absorb other peoples into its own political and religious structures. Historians believe this political and religious imperialism occurred with the Achaemenid Persian Empire (550–330 BCE) and the Sassanian Persian Empire (100–600 CE) with Zoroastrianism as the imperial faith, and the various Arabic Empires (630–1918) with Islam. Jan Assmann believes that in the fourteenth-century BCE Pharaoh Akhenaton created an apparent form of "intolerant monotheism" with the cult of the sun god, Aton, with religious and political imagery of universal dominion of the Egyptian Empire in western Asia (Assmann, 1997: 153). Assmann observes that in the famous Aton Hymn "the rays of the sun embrace all lands and bind them to the submission of the king, a change which obviously translates an imperialistic concept of universal rule into cosmic imagery" (Assmann, 1997: 178). Emperor Constantine of Rome in the fourth century CE may have used Christianity to rule a united Roman Empire and marshal its resources in a great war of conquest against Sassanian Persia (Fowden, 1993; Harris 1995: 164). Jonathan Kirsch chronicled how monotheism came to power in fourth-century CE Rome under Constantine and Theodosius and how under these emperors it manifested its "dark side." For him, this implies that monotheism promotes intolerance in contrast to the tolerance and diversity enjoined by pagan polytheism (Kirsch, 2004). But Kirsh overlooks that Constantinian Christianity was only one form of Christian expression. Simultaneous to Constantine's actions many people became monks to disavow the political compromise of their religion by the Roman Empire. This form of Christian imperialism has been used throughout European history up through western colonial expansion into the Third World. (Otherwise, his popularly written book is marred by a number of factual errors outside his area of expertise.) All of these authors have pointed out that monotheism has been used by autocrats to undergird their tyranny, but that does not discredit monotheism, it only shows how tyrants can manipulate thought to their own benefit. One could say that science should be condemned because the Nazis used sophisticated science to create their death camps.

A more balanced discussion would admit that monotheism, like any intellectual movement, can produce a wide range of social results, both good and bad. Thus, some authors, who engage in a discussion of whether monotheism inherently produces imperialism, tyranny, violence, and patriarchal sexism, suggest that these bad results are aberrations of monotheistic faiths. They believe that monotheism in general introduces both intolerance and openness into the communities through which it spreads, depending upon who is responsible for articulating that faith and bringing it to the masses (Petersen, 1988: 92–107; various essays in Geffré et al., 1985; Michaels, 1994: 51–7; Gross, 1999: 349–55 et passim).

State-sponsored monotheism most likely will emphasize the monarchical aspects of the one deity and the corresponding legitimacy of monarchy. State-sponsored monotheism uses the analogy of one God in the heavens ruling all people, which corresponds to one monarch on the earth ruling all his (or her) subjects. This is monotheism "from above," a religion imposed upon the subjects by the elite to legitimate their power. Such a religion has the "Mosaic Distinction," as Jan Assman calls it, the proclivity to recall the religion of one's opponents, especially polytheists, as idolatry, while one's own religion is the truth (Assmann, 1997). Assmann believes that this typifies what Akhenaton of Egypt did in the fourteenth century BCE for political reasons. This first monotheism or proto-monotheism was blatantly inspired "from above" by Pharaoh Akhenaton, who may have equated himself with Aton, the sun god, so as to solidify his grip on power against the Amon priesthood. Imperial monotheisms have arisen ever since and will continue until the spirit of "real monotheism" or "monotheism from below" unfolds in human society to undercut such oppressive religion. I have adopted the expressions "monotheism from above" and "monotheism from below" from Gerd Theissen's writings (Theissen, 1985).

Monotheism that takes root among poor, marginal, oppressed people, such as the ancient Jews or early Christians, sees one God alone in the heavens implying that all people ought to worship that one deity and stand as equals before that one deity. This monotheism will be critical of kings and kingship, as I have detailed in an earlier work (Gnuse, 2011). An ideology undergirded by "monotheism from above" puts the king into a more direct relationship with God, and leaves the common folk dependent upon the king's relationship to the divine for their well being. Monotheism of the common folk, however, rejects the exaltation of a mere human being to divine or semi-divine status. This is monotheism "from below," from the people. Some scholars will argue that the monotheism of the Jews was brought to the masses by kings, scribes, and priestly elite. Prior to the exile, reforms of Hezekiah (710–700 BCE) and Josiah (625–609 BCE) implemented rather coercive methods to accomplish what appears to be monotheistic reform. In the post-exilic era, the efforts of Ezra, with his exclusion of foreign wives, appears rather authoritarian. These reforms might appear to be a "monotheism from above," actions ultimately mandated by Judean kings to fend off Assyria, or the Persian Empire to make Judah a bulwark against Egyptian expansion.

However, pre-exilic Judahite and post-exilic Jewish political and priestly leadership must still be accounted as part of the oppressed, small powers in the arena of gargantuan political forces, even when their religious reform was sponsored by those foreign powers (as with Ezra and Nehemiah). Hezekiah, Josiah, Nehemiah, Ezra, and nameless others attempted to enable their people to survive; they were not ruling an empire in the name of their religion. They were the oppressed seeking to survive. They were indeed people working "from below" and not "from above," like the Assyrian and Persian rulers. Their efforts give rise to a "religion from below," a religion of the subjugated peoples. This form of religion of the people, "the religion from below" will survive over the years, while the "religion" or "monotheism from above" fades away when the empire collapses. A "religion from below" is rooted in people, and people endure; but a "religion from above" is rooted in a powerful but transitory empire.

A variation on the critique of monotheism comes from Paul Ciholas, who views the Old Testament monotheism as violent but the New Testament monotheism as just and affirming. Ciholas compares Old Testament or Mosaic monotheism with its absolute and jealous deity who promotes violence, unlike pagan philosophical monotheism which seeks to overcome violence, and Christianity which seeks the unity of all people by proclaiming the death of Jesus as the end of violence, including religious violence (Ciholas, 1981: 325–54). Ciholas' message is noble, but his understanding of the Hebrew Bible is shallow and inadequate. Ciholas does not understand that in the Old Testament behind the judgment there is the image of a gracious God who forgives and restores.

Polytheism or Monotheism?

Polytheism has been compared to monotheism as a religiosity that encourages toleration because of its acceptance of diversity in the divine realm, whereas monotheism breeds intolerant devotion to one deity and the commitment desire to convert others. This is best expressed in the writings of Alain de Benoist (de Benoist, 1977, 1981), whose ideas are critiqued by André Dumas (Dumas, 1985: 81–90). This movement among intellectuals has been termed neo-paganism.

Neo-paganism advocates believe that recognizing various divine forces rather than a single deity, can acknowledge the truth to be found in all the world's religions. If many gods are operative in the universe, then believers may live diverse life-styles because each person is free from the harsh demands of one god. This will create greater toleration in our modern world. Monotheism demands submission of the will to one god, but polytheism permits greater diversity and human individuality. Supposedly this typified the culture of the late Roman Empire (Marquard, 1979: 40–58; Veyne, 1987: 216; Fowden, 1993: 37–60). If monotheists worship one universal deity and reject the religion of others, it means that the fight for a particular religion and deity vitiates the idea of a universal and loving God of all people (Comblin, 1985: 91–9). Hellenistic philosophical monotheisms and Hindu monism both demonstrated a toleration of religious diversity (Duquoc, 1985: 61).

But you can also turn this argument around in another direction. Rodney Stark points out that polytheisms with their many gods do not make demands of people, but the "immense Gods of the monotheisms ask much more and get it." These requests by the monotheistic Gods include significant moral codes. This will bring about the emergence of a higher morality and impera- tive to social justice. Stark makes this observation in the context of observing how Christianity with its stern moral code and its appeal to God generated opposition to slavery early on in its history and inspired abolitionist movements in the eighteenth and nineteenth centuries in Britain and America (Stark, 2013: 324–5). In response to the neo-pagans we could say that monotheism declares that if there is one God, and people are children of that one God, then monotheistic believers need to treat all people with respect. That is, in fact, what many texts in the New Testament declare.

One might also observe in human history that polytheisms did not always bring peace, harmony, and universal toleration. In the ancient world, especially Mesopotamia, city states and nations went to war proclaiming that their victory was a victory of their city state deity or deity of the empire against the gods of the enemies. Often, conquering nations, like the Assyrians, would defeat a people and seize the statues of the gods from their temples to take them back to the homeland of the empire. There the gods of the conquered nations would supposedly revere the supreme god of the conquerors. Polytheism also legitimated war and conquest in the hands of power-hungry rulers. It was this rhetoric that goaded the Jews into monotheism, for they had to listen to the propaganda that Marduk of Babylon had defeated Yahweh of Judah. No, toleration is not an inherently quality of polytheism. The problem is not with religion; it is with people.

Sometimes Christians compromise their principle of universal human love for certain advantages in the social and political realm. Constantine and other emperors used Christianity for political purposes, even though that did not reflect the spirit of Christianity. Christians in the days of Constantine supported his actions, for it helped end the persecutions and spread their faith throughout the empire and strengthen the institutional church. Oh yes, and sometimes rewards were given to clerics from the governmental leaders for their cooperation. Ever since Constantine, Christians too often have been willing to allow political leaders to use the Christian faith for repression in return for political favors for the institutional church. We have seen this in Nazi Germany, Communist Eastern Europe, and Latin America. Christians must be aware of the frequent oppressive use of their religion by scheming political leaders against other people. Jürgen Moltmann has noted that if religious monotheism combines with absolutism in the church and state, tyranny results, then only atheism can rescue the human freedom that Christianity once proclaimed (Moltmann, 1985: 51).

Monotheistic Suppression of Women?

Somewhat related to the neo-pagan debate is the accusation that monotheism leads to the suppression of women. Monotheisms portray God as masculine and thus exclude the feminine from the divine realm. When that one deity demands that all people worship "him," the other gods are slowly eliminated. But the last deities to go are the female ones held most precious in the homes by women, due to their contribution to female fertility and food production, and so they receive the greatest monotheistic critique. Consider Asherah in the Old Testament; she was the last to go and probably the hardest to "kill." She finally was turned into an abstraction, the Law, Wisdom, the shekinah, etc., in the final stages of her elimination. All of those were feminine words and by personifying them almost into divine forces, Asherah was replaced. She survives as Mary in popular Roman Catholic piety, proving the need for a feminine dimension in the divine realm. Monotheistic faiths tended to exclude high priestesses, the representatives of the female gods, from worship.

Some scholars believe that the polytheistic faiths with their female deities were more tolerant of women in the cult. Marija Gimbutas, in her study of primitive religion, suggests that originally religions elevated the mother goddess, but with the rise of a patriarchal religion, there came the subordination of women (Gimbutas, 1974). There is much truth in this, especially in the fourth and third millennium BCE of Mesopotamian history. With the rise of warfare after 2600 BCE over precious land and water resources, the Mesopotamians focused more on male gods of war than female goddesses of fertility. However, it should be challenged whether polytheism or a mother goddess oriented religion gave women dignity in the ancient world. The cults of Inanna/Ishtar in Mesopotamia and Isis in Egypt had women votaries, but the status of women was still very poor in both those societies, and male leadership prevailed (Gerstenberger, 2007: 93). Polytheistic societies did not challenge the patriarchal assumptions in those cultures.

In fertility religions with a supreme female goddess, a young woman might obtain a respectful position as a priestess. One fortunate lady ultimately becomes the high priestess, but the others do not. If the role of priestesses may have involved sexual activity in the cult in both ancient Near and the Mediterranean world, such advancement is hardly ennobling. Most women in society did not become priestesses; they remained subordinate to their patriarchal husbands. Polytheistic religions with goddesses did not liberate them, for not all women could become the high priestess.

Veneration of Asherah in the Old Testament was a mode of pious expression for women in their homes. Jeremiah condemns the actions of women baking Asherah cakes (Jer 44:15–19). The Asherah cult was a private woman's religion in the home, and being limited to the home it tended to acknowledge the inferior status of women. By way of contrast, a monotheistic faith eventually grants more dignity to women by including them in the public worship (as Christianity did) rather then indirectly limiting them to a private cult at home.

But what really caused the subordination of women in ancient Israel? Did the religion subordinate women primarily? Did emergent monotheism subordinate women? Or were women subordinate in a patriarchal society before Yahwism arose? I would say the subordination of women existed before monotheism, and that monotheism really helped ameliorate the low status of women by seeking to give them more rights. A consideration of the biblical laws will bear this point out. Pre-existing patriarchalism was so strong in society before Yahwistic monotheism that it would take years to lessen this patriarchy. (We still fight for women's rights today.) State structures and social organization, including temple hierarchies, created patriarchalism in society. In the early second millennium BCE Hammurabi's laws indicate that women were property of men, and their sexual behavior was regulated by legal laws and customs because of their child-bearing capacity and thus the ability to create heirs who would inherit the family wealth. Do not blame monotheism for the subordination of women; it existed millennia before Yahwistic monotheism. The rise of the Assyrian and Babylonian Empires in the eighth through the sixth centuries BCE brought economic oppression to Israelites and Judahites, so that marginal people, including women, were hurt the most. Last of all, priestly assumptions about female impurity connected to menstruation existed before monotheism. The biblical text recalls those phenomena because they were the generic assumptions of other contemporary cultures (Lerner, 1986: 88–91). Once monotheism arose, old values from the prior age still endured. Monotheism cannot change society and the minds of people immediately, especially in matters of the home and the family.

The subordination of women continued through the history of Christianity because the evolution of biblical values takes time to unfold. It takes longer to radically change family values than social or economic values. The biblical tradition does not subordinate women, when it reflects the subordination of women; it portrays the culture of that age. For two millennia men quoted the Bible to subordinate women, but they failed to see those texts that declare the equality of all people before God. When the Bible characterizes God as masculine, it is because there is only one deity, and you cannot assign sex to different divine beings as you once did. However, at times in the Old Testament God is metaphored as both masculine and feminine, a sign that the metaphor of gender is only symbolic. Erhard Gerstenberger said:

> I find untenable an attempt to reconstruct a direct monocausal relationship between the rise of monotheism in Israel and the denigration of women … belief in God includes the greatest possible openness to the justified claims of equality of all people. (Gerstenberger, 2007: 94, 110)

Gerda Lerner noted that it was tragic that monotheism emerged in a society with strong patriarchy, for the religious belief then unfortunately affirmed that patriarchy in many ways (Lerner, 1986: 198). That is true, but monotheism also planted the seeds to undercut that patriarchy ultimately.

Monotheisms "From Above" and "From Below"

Many different forms of monotheistic religious expression exist among believers, even within the same religious tradition simultaneously. Devotees may affirm human equality, dignity, toleration, and peace, and at the same time other adherents of the faith use the religion to justify imperial conquest. Already in the fourth century CE people were moved to reject the Roman patronage of their Christian religion, and they became monks. The piety of medieval monks, like St. Francis, existed alongside medieval rulers who sought to aggrandize power in the name of the same religion. Gentle Sufi mystics like Rumi, Abu-Yazid, and Al-Hallaj co-existed in Islam with powerful Abbasid caliphs in Baghdad. The historian of religion must determine whose faith and actions truly represent the beliefs of the faith and the sacred texts that undergird those religions. Some might say that we should consider the actions of all the religious adherents; others would say that only those faithful to the spirit of the religious tradition represent the faith. I believe in the latter definition and would affirm that those who represent the faith best are those who are most faithful to the spirit of the original message of the founding spokespersons and the sacred texts. Religious spokespersons must be grounded in their texts and traditions to maintain continuity with the core values of their faith. Sensitive religious leaders over the years, such as St. Francis, criticized their societies and especially the leaders for betraying the deeper values of the religious tradition.

Rodney Stark generated a penetrating analysis of monotheistic faiths to undercut facile generalizations people have made about monotheism and the western religions. He maintains that monotheists will be aggressive in general because they believe that they hold ultimate truth. He believes that "particularism" is inherent in monotheisms. Monotheisms promote conflict between theological factions within the religion and conflict with other religions. Yet the pattern of this aggression varies over the years and in various countries. Jews were persecuted by both Christians and Muslims equally (even in supposedly tolerant Spain under Muslim rule). Closer examination shows that persecution was almost non-existent from 500 to 1000 CE and then became intense during the years from 1000 to 1500 CE. When Islam and Christianity were in conflict with each other, religionists in Christian Europe and Muslim Spain and the Middle East became determined to purge the unfaithful, and Jews suffered.

Monotheisms are intolerant when they are in a period of stress or in competition with another religion or ideology. But when there are various competing religious systems, such as in the United States, monotheisms are more tolerant, since they are in no position to dominate society (Stark, 2001: 31–259). In another work Stark maintains that the zeal of monotheism undergirded opposition to slavery throughout history. He criticizes historians who downplay the historic critique against slavery found in Christian circles, not only after the fall of Rome and throughout the Middle Ages and early modern period, but especially in the modern era. He notes how the Roman Catholic church sought to oppose slavery in the sixteen century and how religious rhetoric among Protestants generated the abolitionist movement in the eighteenth and nineteenth centuries. Only in Christian circles did abolitionism emerge (Stark, 2013: 291–365). In my opinion Stark has unveiled the nature of triumphal monotheisms, rather than all monotheisms. His examples of intolerant Islam and Christianity are those historical situations in which the religion and the social-political values of the government were tightly intertwined. He often points out how persecution occurred as a result of popular activity of the masses against the will of their governments, and that the official leaders of the church, such as bishops, often desperately attempted to stem the tide of persecution. Again, I would say that the religious elites understood the message of the faith and realized that such oppressive behavior was wrong, while the masses, being poorly educated, had come to connect their religious values with their own social-political, economic, national agenda, and personal frustrations. Stark has also unveiled how the zeal of monotheism can create social justice, especially in regard to the issue of abolishing slavery. Stark has truly seen the complexity of monotheistic thought and its social-political connections.

Some interpretations of monotheism are imperialistic and others proclaim a message of peace and human unity. There are monotheisms "from above," defined by a monarch, pharaoh, emperor, or tyrant, who uses the religions for their own political purposes, and there are monotheisms "from below," from the people crying for dignity, toleration, and peace. In a polytheistic worldview, such as in the ancient Near East, wars between nations reflected the wars in the heavens between the gods, but theoretically belief in one God should end wars and oppression (Theissen, 1985: 71). It takes time, perhaps centuries, for the majority of religionists in a monotheistic faith to perceive that human dignity and rights are intended for all people equally in a way that moves beyond the beliefs and practices of the cultures in which that monotheism arose.

All three monotheistic religions proclaim human equality, toleration, and a vision of peace. Cultures touched by those religious traditions have provided increased egalitarian expressions over the years. When religion is no longer used to justify war, imperialism, conquest, and as the apology of one race of people for enslaving another race (to quote Lincoln), then monotheism will have actualized one of the most significant components of its ideological matrix. We will look back and see that imperialistic monotheisms were an evolutionary dead end in monotheistic development. Monotheisms "from below," which unite people by the power of the human spirit rather than by the sword, will be seen as the true heirs to the monotheistic breakthrough in the biblical tradition.

Some Conclusions

Biblical scholars affirm that the monotheism of the Old Testament and the New Testament does not legitimate political empire, but rather encourages solidarity with all of humanity. The believers who generated these texts were often the oppressed and victims of political systems in their own age. For example, the prophets spoke of a universal deity who would bring a state of peace and prosperity to all people someday (Lang, 1983: 55; Theissen, 1985: 71; Albertz, 1994b: 2, 425; Dietrich, 1994: 2–7). The following oracle is found in both Mic 4:3–4 and Isa 2:4:

> "He shall judge between the nations, and shall arbitrate for many peoples; they shall beat their swords into plowshares and their spears into pruning hooks; nation shall not lift up sword against nation, neither shall they learn war anymore, but they shall all sit under their own vines and under their own fig trees, and no one shall make them afraid."

This oracle comes "from below," from the voice of a defeated and conquered people under the heels of the Assyrian Empire. This prophetic text expresses hope in overcoming war between people by the recognition that there is only one God over all humanity. This is an oracle reflecting religious faith "from below," even if the prophetic author, Isaiah or Micah, was not yet a monotheist in the fullest sense, but was evolving in that direction. In the polytheism of the ancient Near East the wars between peoples reflected the wars in the heavens between the gods, but the emergence of one God should spell the end of wars and oppression as well as creating a vision of all people as equals under that one deity (Theissen, 1985: 71). Perhaps the spirit of this prophetic oracle has yet to permeate the consciousness of believers in those faiths. There is an evolutionary trajectory in the monotheistic process that is still seeking to come to fruition. The monotheistic breakthrough of ancient Israel is still unfolding, and we are still in the formative stages.

In conclusion, authors have pointed out that monotheism has occasioned repressive behavior in history, including the suppression of women. However,

I believe the role of monotheism and oppressive political and religious behavior has to be described in more nuanced fashion. We need to distinguish between what monotheistic faiths should do, that is, create egalitarianism, as opposed to how monotheistic faiths have been used by political powers to create oppression. Thus, it is useful to employ metaphors which speak of "monotheisms from above" as opposed to "monotheisms from below." Monotheisms true to the spirit of the founders or the primal original texts are "monotheisms from below," which encourage the eventual development of egalitarianism. I believe that monotheism, especially the Judeo-Christian tradition, is on an evolutionary trajectory, ever unfolding the egalitarian implications of its own message. Over the years the Judeo-Christian tradition will increasingly seek to affirm human dignity and equality.

2 The Prophets Demand Justice on Behalf of "The One God"

Programmatic Biblical Statements

Some scholars and critics have declared that monotheism breeds intolerance and supports tyranny and authoritarianism. In my opinion the best response is the Hebrew Bible. For within the pages of this canonical document we observe literature that affirms the exclusive worship of one God and a call for justice in society. This is most particularly evident in the prophetic oracles of pre-exilic prophets and the law codes found in Exodus 21–23, Deuteronomy 12–26, and the laws in Leviticus. The call to worship one God and to promote justice in society is intertwined in much of this literature. The biblical text does not explain how the exclusive worship of one God is organically connected to the call for social justice, but then people of that age did not engage in that kind of reflective intellectual activity that appeals to us today. Thus, authors can challenge the idea that exclusive worship or even stricter monotheism is connected to the call for social justice. But in my mind the fact remains that these two messages are intertwined in the literature of the prophets and the laws. Furthermore, I would say, if we step back and consider the canon as a whole, these two messages have been raised to a level of official belief by the Jewish and the Christian community. The literature lies before us as an authoritative text demanding exclusive devotion to one God and justice in society. Let us then consider some of this literature.

Before we turn our attention to the prophets it must be stated that there are biblical texts that virtually scream monotheism and social justice in the same sentences.

My eye is drawn especially to the powerful statements in Psalm 82 where the poet rhapsodically declares that Yahweh killed the other gods because they were unjust and did not help the poor. How much more dramatic can it be said? Monotheism and social justice are connected. Hear the words of Ps 82:1–8:

(1) God has taken his place in the divine council; in the midst of the gods he holds judgment:

(2) "How long will you judge unjustly and show partiality to the wicked?

(3) Give justice to the weak and the orphan; maintain the right of the lowly and the destitute.

(4) Rescue the weak and the needy; deliver them from the hand of the wicked."

(5) They have neither knowledge nor understanding, they walk around in darkness, all the foundations of the earth are shaken.

(6) I say, "You are gods, children of the Most High, all of you;

(7) Nevertheless, you shall die like mortals, And fall like any prince."

(8) Rise up, O God, judge the earth; For all the nations belong to you!

The gods must die because they have no sense of social justice, leaving only one deity in the divine realm – Yahweh.

Genesis 1 is accorded the honor of being a paean to monotheism, declaring the majestic power of God in creating the world. But it is not mentioned enough that within these six days of creation there is an incredibly powerful statement of human equality, human nobility, and the equality of the sexes. Hear the words of Gen 1:26–27:

> (26) Then God said, "Let us make humankind in our image, according to our likeness; and let them have dominion over the fish of the sea, and over the birds of the air, and over the cattle, and over all the wild animals of the earth, and over every creeping thing that crawls upon the earth" (27). So God created humankind in his image, in the image of God he created them; male and female he created them.

The words "rule" (radah), "image" (selem), and "likeness" (demuth) are words used to describe kings, as their Babylonian cognates even more clearly indicate: "rule" (radati), "image" (salmu), and "likeness" (demuti) in texts from Mesopotamia. The man and the woman are royalty, and their descendants are all kings and queens. This is an incredibly ennobling view of all of humanity. Furthermore, this is true of both men and women equally. Verse 27 clearly states that both the male and the female are created in the royal image of God. When the famous preacher John Ball preached this passage from the pulpit in London in 1381 he helped inspire the famous "Peasants Revolt" of 1381. The Bible contains dangerous texts for tyrants (Gnuse, 2011).

Yet again, let us turn to the New Testament. In Gal 3:28 Paul boldly declares:

> "There is no longer Jew or Greek, there is no longer slave or free, there is no longer male and female; for all of you are one in Christ Jesus."

Paul is not describing heaven, as I was taught as a child, he is very clearly talking about the here and now in the Christian community. Paul boldly declares the equality of slaves with their masters. What a dangerous thing to say in the Roman Empire. Paul declares the equality of men and women. What a dangerous thing to say in that patriarchal age in the east Mediterranean world. That would be dangerous to say even today. What is true for the Christian community from the writings of Paul would in time be seen as true for society, and we still struggle today to bring Paul's vision for humanity to fruition. I have addressed how the Bible actually speaks a liberating word in that ancient society on behalf of both slaves and women (Gnuse, 2015b).

If we believe that these biblical authors actually believed what they said, we must assume that somehow the monotheism they affirmed was somehow intertwined in their minds with human equality and the subsequent social justice that follows upon the values of human equality.

Maybe not all Jews and Christians (especially) have followed the message of these texts, but the message is clearly there in those texts. I believe that a religion should be understood and evaluated by what its texts declare and not by what some idiots have done with that religion over the years. People too often use their religion to justify the evil things that they wished to do, and they have not really listened to the texts or the message of their religion. Critical scholars in the previous section have too often evaluated monotheistic faiths on the basis of what the tyrants have done. If the Nazis used science to brutally murder millions of people in their death camps, do we then condemn science?

Prophets Call for Justice on Behalf of the One God

If we wish to see dramatic words from the biblical text that speak out on behalf of both monotheism and social justice for the oppressed, the best place to look is the prophetic literature in the Old Testament. The prophets most assuredly spoke out and demanded that the Israelites should worship only Yahweh and not the other gods. No one can deny that. But mingled in with their call for the exclusive worship of Yahweh is biting invective speaking out on behalf of the poor. They do not explicate for us how these two themes are connected, but they are clearly intertwined in their prophetic oracles.

The failure to worship Yahweh exclusively and the call for justice was one of the themes of the pre-exilic prophets who condemned Israelite and Judahite societies for the sins and threatened them with divine punishment. Their oracles were recalled probably by scribes during the Babylonian Exile (586–539 BCE) and thereafter to justify why the nation was destroyed in 586 BCE. Most likely, many oracles were crafted and added to the prophetic books by those scribes, and scholars have debated which oracles were added. Some commentators suppose only minimal additions were made to certain prophetic books, other commentators surmise that the bulk of a particular prophetic book may come from the hands of those later exilic and post-exilic scribes. Either way we have the testimony from that ancient time when monotheism began to emerge that social justice and the exclusive worship of one deity are intimately connected.

The purpose for recalling such grim prophetic utterances was to say that the judgment of the past has been fulfilled; now the faithful await the future hope of restoration and even glorification. The judgment oracles were a foil for the messages of the hope oracles. It must also be said that the Babylonian Exile for most Jews lasted well beyond the return of the first small group that came back after 539 BCE. Thus, "exilic literature" could be crafted down to the Hellenistic era for those "exiled" Jews. In this regard, I include the final work Priestly Editors (perhaps 400 BCE or later) as "exilic literature." Thus, as we look at pre-exilic prophets, we must admit the possibility that oracles were added down to the Maccabean era.

In a perusal of prophets such as Amos, Hosea, Micah, Isaiah, Jeremiah, and Ezekiel, ostensibly the pre-exilic prophets who contain judgment oracles, we observe that the vast portion of their invective is directed against people for failure to worship Yahweh exclusively. Clearly exclusive worship of Yahweh or maybe even monotheism is most central to their concerns. But let us attend to hearing their cries for justice that accompany this message. It appears that they may be saying an exclusive devotion to Yahweh will lead believers to practice justice in society and to attend to the needs of the poor. In Deuteronomy the authors clearly and repeatedly declare that the awareness of how God saved them in the exodus should lead listeners to attend to the needs of the poor, recalling that once they were slaves in Egypt. Deuteronomy was crafted after most of the pre-exilic prophets spoke, but might we suggest that such a thought was latent in those earlier prophets.

Amos was the first of those whom we call the classical prophets. It is suggested that he was not a monotheist. His message was one of social criticism primarily; his oracles can help reconstruct how the rich took advantage of the poor in the middle of the eighth century BCE, so he did not speak as much to religious issues as did Hosea. He warned Israelites in the northern state that they would fall to the Assyrians in war, but Amos is remembered today as "the prophet of justice for the poor" (Houston 2006: 73).

In his famous "Day of the Lord" oracle in the first two chapters of the book, he uttered the famous words in Amos 2:6–7:

> "because they sell the righteous for silver, and the needy for a pair of sandals – they who trample the head of the poor into the dust of the earth, and push the afflicted out of the way."

So many people had been dispossessed of their land by the rich, that there were tremendous numbers of debt slaves, and thus a debt slave could be purchased for the price of a pair of sandals. Though some scholars think the image of sandals refers to the small debt owed by the peasant that forced him into slavery (Harper, 1904: 49), or the passing of a pair of sandals in a business transaction, and here it would refer to the transaction in which a poor person is bound over into debt slavery (Mays, 1969: 45; Andersen and Freedman, 1989: 312). In Amos 8:4–6, the prophet decries how this impoverishment occurred:

> "Hear this, you that trample on the needy, and bring to ruin the poor of the land.... We will make the ephah small and the shekel great, and practice deceit with false balances, buying the poor for silver and the needy for a pair of sandals, and selling the sweeping of the wheat."

The rich used two sets of scales to buy low and sell high when dealing with customers, and even putting the refuse of the gleaning process in the baskets for sale. They especially sell high to the landless peasants who have already lost their farms due to dishonest business practices (Mays, 1969: 143). Before legislation in Deuteronomy a merchant could actually use a scale one ephah smaller than the standard weight (Mays, 1976: 146).

Amos, in general, attacks the oppressive actions of royal officials who impoverish the poor in Amos 5:11–12:

> "Therefore, because you trample on the poor and take from them levies of rain ... you who afflict the righteous, who take a bribe, and push aside the needy in the gate."

Israel's representatives of the king overtaxed the peasants, took bribes to exempt the rich, and judges received bribes and did not render justice verdicts in the city gate where trials were held (Mays, 1969: 94). In the middle of the eighth century BCE in the northern state of Israel, the rich were richer than before and the peasants were impoverished by dishonest business tactics, fell into debt slavery, lost their land, and became servants in the homes of the rich. As a result, when war with Assyria came, peasants who fought in the armies did not fight passionately, and the country was defeated and conquered by Assyria.

Amos seems to imply that the state religion permitted this social abuse by focusing on cult and ritual rather than justice in society.

Hosea is often perceived by scholars as being closer to some form of monotheism than Amos. Hosea's religious critique was also contemporary with Amos' social message, and it provides the other side of the story. The royal cult in Bethel, focused upon the calf, was a sacerdotal religion emphasizing fertility, and subsequently turning the attention of the worshippers away from social values of traditional highland Yahwism. Hosea also spoke to people in the northern state of Israel but for a longer period of time than Amos, perhaps down to and even beyond the destruction of Samaria and the nation of Israel in 722 BCE.

In the southern state of Judah Isaiah functioned as a prophet in the royal court of Ahaz and Hezekiah in the later eighth century BCE. Perhaps he had been a priest prior to his prophetic calling, hence his presence in the Temple for that call. In his early oracles he attacks the social and economic abuses in Judah, which were similar to those up in the north, in Israel. In the early chapters of the book, which may come from early in his career, we hear him utter an imperative to justice in positive terms. In Isa 1:17 he says:

> "learn to do good; seek justice, rescue the oppressed, defend the orphan, plead for the widow."

Elsewhere he criticizes the ruthless actions of the rich, as in Isa 3:14b-15:

> "It is you who have devoured the vineyard; the spoil of the poor is in your houses. What do you mean by crushing my people, by grinding the face of the poor."

He subsequently says that God will bring the Assyrians to punish Israel for their social injustice. If no one will help the poor, God will act (Kaiser, 1972: 30). In a polytheistic cosmos, no one God would act so dramatically, but when there is one deity in the divine realm, dramatic actions can be taken using foreign peoples, who once used to belong to other gods. Monotheism can make the plea for social justice more dramatic.

And again in Isa 10:2 the prophet proclaims:

> "to turn aside the needy from justice and to rob the poor of many people of their right, that widows may be your spoil, and that you make the orphans your prey!"

This might refer to new unjust laws issued by King Ahaz or unjust court decisions (Oswalt, 1986: 259). Laws can be "legal" but unjust, just as in our world today (Clements, 1980: 61–2). These judgment oracles, presumably given early in his career, were under King Ahaz. During the Assyrian crisis (710–701 BCE) Isaiah was more the prophet of hope declaring that Jerusalem would be spared from the Assyrian war machine. Hence, we have no social critique in those later oracles.

In those later years Isaiah, who lived in Jerusalem, had a country contemporary, Micah. Micah proclaimed a message of judgment against the rich and the powerful on behalf of the poor in the rural villages where he lived. His descriptions of the oppression parallel what Amos said. In Mic 2:2 we hear:

> "They covet fields and seize them; houses, and take them away; they oppress householder and house, people and their inheritance."

In Mic 6:11-12a we hear, "Can I tolerate wicked scales and a bag of dishonest weight? Your wealthy are full of violence."

The rich again manipulated the economy to put the peasants at disadvantage until they became debt slaves and lost their land to the rich. If a family lost their land, they lost their independence, and if they were not initially debt slaves, they would quickly become such (Mays, 1976: 64).

Jeremiah lived a century later in Judah and prophesied after the Deuteronomic Reform movement had flourished (622–609 BCE) and floundered after the death of King Josiah in 609 BCE. He was a Deuteronomic reform advocate in an age when many felt this message was no longer valid. Thus, his was a difficult mission. One can hear his cry for the rights of the dispossessed and poor among his many oracles. As in the days of Amos the powerful waxed fat with illegal business practices, using different scales for buying and selling. In his Temple Oracle Jeremiah proclaims a message with language similar to that in Deuteronomy, thus Jer 7:6-7a:

> "if you do not oppress the alien, the orphan, and the widow, or shed innocent blood in this place, and if you do not go after other gods to your hurt, then I will dwell with you in this place."

Jeremiah directed specific judgment oracles against kings for their unjust treatment of the poor. To the king he spoke the following in Jer 22:3:

> "And do no wrong or violence to the alien, the orphan, and the widow, or shed innocent blood in this place."

To the king who built his splendid palace by abusing laborers, he spoke thus in Jer 22:13:

> "Woe to him who builds his house by unrighteousness and his upper rooms by injustice; who makes his neighbors work for nothing, and does not give them their wages."

In a longer tirade in Jer 34:13–22 the prophet inveighs against King Zedekiah for violating the Sabbath Year debt slave release guidelines of Deuteronomy 15 by taking back his slaves after once releasing them. This appears to be a clear reference to one of the Deuteronomic reform laws proclaimed in the generation prior. The destruction of Jerusalem in 586 BCE vindicated Jeremiah's message of warning but signaled his defeat as a prophet who sought to save his people from such a destruction. Though he might have deemed his ministry a failure, his words have been recalled for over 2,000 years.

Ezekiel lived in the Babylonian Exile, having been dragged there in the first capture of Jerusalem by the Babylonians in 597 BCE. Thus, he spoke oracles both before and after the 586 BCE destruction of the city. Prior to the fall he was a prophet of judgment, after the fall he became a beacon of hope. In his judgment oracles he sought to justify why Jerusalem and Judah were being destroyed, and one of the reasons they faced divine wrath was their oppression of the poor. Ezek 18:5–8 declares:

> "If a man is righteous and does what is lawful and right ... does not oppress anyone, but restores to the debtor his pledge, commits no robbery, gives his bread to the hungry, and covers the naked with a garment, does not take advance or accrued interest, withholds his hand from iniquity, executes true justice between contending parties.

In this passage Ezekiel states positively what often prophets condemn negatively, and as we shall see, are issues addressed by reforming laws (Bills, 2020: 47). Ezekiel spoke to a Jewish audience after they lost a horrible war, and his particular audience were exiles in Babylon. To economically oppress your fellow Jews in those distressful circumstances was particularly odious (Weaver, 1969: 110; Eichrodt, 1970: 239). Like the pre-exilic prophets, this exilic prophet also decries dramatically the worship of other gods alongside Yahweh and the unjust treatment of the poor.

The prophets affirmed the exclusive worship of Yahweh and the just treatment of the weak and the poor. The message of monotheism and social justice are tightly connected in their proclamations. For me this is the most significant argument to maintain that exclusive worship of one god or monotheism are connected to social justice. The prophets never explain the relationship of these two messages, they simply assume the connection. We must ponder that.

The message of the prophets may be summarized in one verse, which ironically comes from the Psalm (or should I say appropriately?). Ps 140:12 declares:

"I know that the Lord maintains the cause of the needy, and executes justice for the poor."

One God in the heavens declares that all people belong to him/her, and thus they are equal and equally deserving justice.

3 Laws Seek Justice on Behalf of "The One God"

Reforming Law Codes

The economic abuses decried by the prophets appear to be addressed in many of the reforming laws found in the law codes. We particularly observe this in the laws of the Book of the Covenant (Exodus 21–23), the Deuteronomic Laws (Deuteronomy 12-26), and the Priestly Laws (Leviticus). For the past two centuries scholars have noted that the Deuteronomic Laws appear to be a later expansion and development of the Book of the Covenant, which in some cases provided even greater protection for the poor and marginal folk of the land. Furthermore, scholars opine, although more subjectively, that the laws in Leviticus are an even later elaboration on some of those laws (though some scholars have argued for a much earlier date for Priestly literature). I personally suggest that the Book of the Covenant may originate in the late 700s BCE under King Hezekiah, the Deuteronomic Laws emerge under King Josiah around 622 BCE, and the Priestly laws arise sometime during the Babylonian Exile or beyond. However, some contemporary critical scholars suggest the exile or the fifth century BCE for the Deuteronomic Laws (Pakkala, 2009: 388–419, 2010: 201–35) and some very critical scholars place the Book of the Covenant likewise late in the exilic era (Van Seters, 2003).

It has also been suggested that all the law codes are post-exilic literary creations by scribal intelligentsia (Knight, 2011). I shall avoid the complexities of this debate, which I have discussed briefly elsewhere (Gnuse, 2015: 20–7). For the sake of the presentation in this volume I will work with the sequence initially mentioned above, for I believe this is the best way to observe the progression of the legal articulations for the rights of the poor and oppressed. Even if I were to accept the later dates for the law codes, the sequence of the three corpora of laws would still be the same, I believe.

Biblical law codes were not actually used in courtrooms; they were theological statements crafted by scribes to be used as public statements or religious propaganda by kings or other leaders as a statement of their piety and quest for justice in the kingdom. The same is true of ancient Near Eastern law codes, such as Hammurabi's law codes. Hammurabi's laws were never quoted in any court cases, but they were used as scribal teaching devices, copied by students (Bottéro, 1982: 409–44; Watson, 1985; Jackson, 1989: 185–202; Berman, 2014:

24; Greengus, 2000: 1:471–2). Perhaps if a student were later to become a judge, the teaching devices he copied as a scribal student might have influenced his decisions. The Book of the Covenant in Exodus 21–23 may have been a public statement by King Hezekiah of Judah about what he believed should be the legal decisions in courts, and likewise the Deuteronomic Law in Deuteronomy 12–26 may have may a strong religious confession by King Josiah of Judah as to what he believed to be the just legal decisions to be rendered. Whether judges actually heeded the king's proclamation, be he Hammurabi, Hezekiah, or Josiah, we do not know. But it is worth stressing that the biblical law codes, like their ancient Near Eastern counterparts, were ideological, political, and theological (as with the biblical materials) statements, perhaps with some intent to change legal decisions in the courts.

That these biblical law codes were theological statements is attested by the presence of religious rhetoric in the codes. Such rhetoric, sometimes expansive, appeals to divine authority for the need to keep these "commands." The laws sometimes appeal especially for the need to care for the alien visitor or stranger, the widow, and the orphan (Exod 22:22; Deut 10:18; 14:29; 24:17, 21; 26; 13), and how Judahites should do this because they ought to remember that they were once slaves and aliens in Egypt redeemed by God (Exod 22:21; 23:9; Deut 10:19; 15:15; 24:18; 26:5–8). It even declares that God will hear the cry of the oppressed and punish the folk of Judah if they fail to help (Exod 22:22; Deut 15:9). This language indicates how this is theological, not legal language.

Foundational Legal Statements

Programmatic statements are sometimes found in the law codes that tell us much about the assumptions of the lawgivers and how they strive for justice in the articulation of these laws. Such a statement is found in Exod 21:23–25, which reveals much if we think about it carefully:

> (23) If any harm follows, then you shall give life for life, (24) eye for eye, tooth for tooth, hand for hand, foot for foot, (25) burn for burn for burn, wound for wound, stripe for stripe.

People who casually refer to this law, the principle of lex talionis, or retributive punishment, often say rather naively that this law reflects the primitive nature of Israelite criminal justice with its brutal physical punishments. Actually, it reflects an incredible egalitarian ethos operative in the laws. First of all, the law says that whatever you do to a person, it could be potentially inflicted upon you by a decision of the elders.

Of course, the court could decide upon a lesser punishment, if mitigating circumstances warranted it. The law declares that all people will receive the same punishment, regardless of their wealth or status in the community. Ancient Near Eastern law codes often inflicted more severe punishments upon the poor who might harm a rich person than the reverse. A poor person who strikes a rich person might be put to death. This biblical law inflicts the same punishment as the crime, thus preventing the rich person from merely paying a fine, which might mean little to him. The rich person could virtually buy his way out of a crime by paying a fine. A poor person assessed the same fine, might be put to death in Mesopotamia, if he were unable to pay the fine. Thus, the biblical law ensures that all, rich and poor, are equal before the law. Second, the law prevents the punishment from being greater than the crime. A crime against a rich person by a poor person could bring a much greater punishment than the crime itself.

This principle caps the punishment so that it is no greater than the crime itself. Third, it should be duly noted that the trial occurs before the elders or in a courtroom. This principle seeks to eliminate private revenge. So often in movies and television a heroic individual goes out to wreak revenge on someone who has wronged him, and he dramatically quotes this passage. On the contrary, this text implies that such grievances are to be brought before the courts, not by personal vendetta (Frankl, 2005: 31).

Another programmatic statement which clearly reflects the agenda of social justice in the law codes is found in Exod 22:21–23:(21)

> You shall not wrong or oppress a resident alien, for you were aliens in the land of Egypt. (22) You shall not abuse any widow or orphan. (23) If you do abuse them, when they cry out to me, I will surely heed their cry.

We see a similar statement later in the same law code, Exod 23:6–8:

> (6) You shall not pervert the justice due to your poor in their lawsuits. (7) Keep far from a false charge, and do not kill the innocent and those in the right, for I will not acquit the guilty. (8) You shall take no bribe, for a bribe blinds the officials, and subverts the cause of those who are in the right. (9) You shall not oppress a resident alien; you know the heart of an alien, for you were aliens in the land of Egypt.

These statements can be found frequently in the law codes of Exodus and Deuteronomy. Individual laws in Deuteronomy which address specific issues often make this appeal especially to help the poor, the widow, the orphan, and the sojourner or resident alien.

Laws on Loans and Debts Evolved

As law codes evolved one can see in the successive codes in Exodus, Deuteronomy, and Leviticus a desire to increasingly assist the poor in their economic struggles. The development of laws regarding debts and debt slaves especially reflects this reforming instinct in the legal tradition, and it also demonstrates their belief in God and the essential equality of all people.

In ancient Israel, as today, people fell into debt, and consequently they obtained loans. But if they could not pay back these loans, they fell into greater financial distress.

Peasant farmers in the highlands brought their surplus crops, usually grain, to cities such as Samaria, to sell their crops, and sometimes other peasants would need to buy agricultural produce if their crop yield was low that year. Merchants were unscrupulous and often would use different weights to buy and to sell the produce to the various peasants. Thus, they brought low and sold high and put the peasants at a financial disadvantage. This was the first step in driving a particular peasant family into financial distress, debt, and debt slavery. Thus, biblical legislators had to address the issue of dishonest weights. Amos mentions this practice as an example of social injustice. In Deut 25:13–15 we see the condemnation of dishonest weights in the marketplace:

> (13) You shall not have in our bag two kinds of weights, large and small. (14) You shall not have in your house two kinds of measures, large and small. (15) You shall have only a full and honest weight; you shall have only a full and honest measure.

Peasants gradually and continually who were cheated in the market place often found themselves forced to take a loan, most likely from one of the merchants who had cheated them. Biblical authors rejected the imposition of interest on loans. Interest could turn borrowers and their families quickly into debt slaves in a simple pastoral and agrarian society, such as Israel and Judah, where most of the debtors were simple farmers. Interest rates in the ancient world averaged around thirty three percent (Houston, 2006: 103–4). The chances for a simple peasant repaying a loan with interest was significantly less than that of a merchant who might receive profit from successful caravan ventures that could reap a 200 percent return. A poor landless person had even less chance to repay. The possibility of loan default was greatest in areas subject to small amounts of rainfall, which included Palestine (Marshall, 1993: 144).

The oldest condemnation of interest is found in the Book of the Covenant, which may be an attempt to mandate economic reform in the face of the economic changes in late-eighth-century BCE Judah. The law reads in Exod 22:25,

> "If you lend money to my people, to the poor among you, you shall not deal with them as a creditor; you shall not exact interest from them."

Expressions, such as "my people" and "the poor," are vocabulary used in the book of Exodus to describe Israelites slaves in Egypt. Subtly the biblical author compares the creditor to pharaoh, who turns the poor into slaves, so that interest can undo the liberation brought about by the exodus (Varso, 2008: 329–31).

Exod 22:26 laid limitations on taking pledges for loans extended to the poor. If a neighbor's cloak was taken in pawn, it had to be returned to him every night. This law implied that other possessions necessary for life had to be returned temporarily or perhaps not borrowed at all.

People circumvented these laws. A loan could be given with an amount taken out of the total sum before the creditor even obtained it. The debtor had to return the full amount with the initial sum or "bite" taken out by the creditor. This "bite" or neshek was not defined as interest, but it forced the debtor to pay back the loan with profit to the creditor. A later law in Deut 23:19–20 condemned this subtle form of interest,

> (19)"You shall not charge interest on loans to another Israelite, interest (neshek) on money, interest (neshek) on provisions, interest (neshek) on anything that is lent. (20) On loans to a foreigner you may charge interest, but on loans to another Israelite you may not charge interest."

Israelite creditors could charge interest on a loan to a foreigner (nokhri), since he was probably a merchant from a foreign country who made a good profit margin in trade (Neufeld, 1955: 359–62, 375–410; Phillips, 1973: 25; Craigie, 1976: 302).Deut 15:7–8 appeals to creditors not to be hard-hearted against the needy, but to lend to meet human need.

Deut 24:6, 10–13, 17 elaborates on items pawned for loans. Creditors are forbidden to take millstones, which are necessary for making bread for a family, and without which the family would fall more quickly into debt. Furthermore, the creditor cannot go into the debtor's house to select an item for collateral, but the debtor must bring out the items for consideration, thus preserving the dignity of a poor person. Any garment taken in pledge must be returned at night, especially for the poor, widows, and orphans.

However, creditors would demand an added amount, not called interest, on a loan, called a tarbith (or marbith). The word was portrayed as a "gift" according to the creditor, thus making tarbith is another way to sidestep the laws against interest, then Leviticus subsequently seeks to stop this practice (Samuel Driver, 1902: 266; ; Stein, 1953: 163; North, 1954: 177; Neufeld, 1955: 357–4; Snaith, 1967: 166; Loewenstamm, 1969: 79–80; Gamoran, 1971: 129–32; Hyatt, 1971: 243; Porter, 1976: 205). In Lev 25:36–37 both the neshek and the tarbith/marbith are condemned,

> (36)Do not take interest (neshek) in advance or otherwise make a profit (tarbith) from them, but fear your God; let them live with you. (37)You

shall not lend them your money at interest (neshek) taken in advance, or
provide them food at a profit (marbith).

There is development through these three texts, as idealistic scribes legislated
on behalf of the poor and oppressed. Though this reflects the simple process that
many laws go through, here we see the purpose is designed to protect the poor
and not just to provide for mere stability in the economic order.

Did the people of Judah and later Jews keep these guidelines? We do not
know whether these biblical texts were scribal creations, unknown to the
average person, or whether they were moral guidelines that people knew
about but did not keep, or whether these were guidelines that Jews did keep at
times. Papyrus records from the Jewish communities in Egypt indicate that
interest was charged on loans from 456 BCE to 221 BCE, but that after 182 BCE
loans were interest-free (Gamoran, 1971: 133–4).

References to debt remission exist from the time of Nehemiah in the fifth
century BCE down to the second century CE (Kessler, 2010: 15–30). At least
some Jews observed these customs, perhaps to preserve their Jewish identity.

Laws on Debt Slaves Evolved

With the development of debt slave laws we see even more the Israelite urge
for social reform. Slave laws evolved to give increased rights to slaves steadily
from the Book of the Covenant, to the Deuteronomic Laws, and finally to
Levitical legislation.

Some scholars believe that the different slave laws covered different situations
and were applied simultaneously, thus there was no evolutionary trajectory in the
laws (Chirichigno, 1993: 17–357). But most scholars view the texts as a historical
development responding to the changing social circumstances of Israelite and
Jewish society. This would be true whether the law codes were used in courtrooms
or whether they were scribal creations by reformers inspired by the prophets.
Ultimately, the slave release laws were grounded in the faith that Yahweh had
saved the Israelites from slavery in Egypt (Exod 22:21; 23:9; Lev 25:42, 55; Deut
15:15).

Jeffries Hamilton uses language similar to mine. Beginning with Deuteronomy
15 biblical manumission slaves laws are a "trajectory" or a "thrust" in history.
Earlier laws permit "subsequent interpreters of the law to build a case for
a broader condemnation of slavery." In Deuteronomy 15 there is a "submerged
condemnation" of slavery that will someday "pose justice questions which even
the text is not willing to pose" to its original audience (Hamilton, 1992: 120–1).
Like him, I believe that these laws lead ultimately to the total condemnation of
slavery for the readers of the text. The monotheistic under-girding behind this
legislation leads to such insights.

In the ancient world slaves arose as prisoners of war and by falling into debt, and in Israel debt accounts for the existence of slaves. Israelites could become slaves in the following ways: children might be sold voluntarily for debts (Exod 21:7–11) or seized for debts (2 Kgs 4:1; Neh 5:5), and adults could be enslaved for debts involuntarily (1 Sam 22:2; Amos 2:6; Isa 50:1) or voluntarily (Exod 21:5–6; Deut 15:16–17).

Inability to repay loans due to high interest rates created many debt slaves. A debtor might lose members of his family into debt slavery, and then eventually he would succumb. This was frequent in Mesopotamia, where economic stagnation or collapse resulted from the large numbers of people who fell into debt slavery and lost their land. Amorite Babylonian kings, including Hammurabi, in the early second millennium BCE issued irregular misharum and anduraru proclamations to release debts and debt slaves to revive an ailing economy and avoid social violence. Biblical authors may have been inspired by Mesopotamian traditions in their creation of Sabbath Year in Deuteronomy and Jubilee Year in Leviticus (Chirichigno, 1993: 30–100). If scribal intelligentsia in Israel learned to write by copying legal Hammurabi's Law Code, among others, this would have inspired them in their construction of law codes. Biblical authors then provided more situations under which slaves could be released. They inspired prophets who called for social justice in the eighth century BCE. In Mesopotamia slaves had no legal protection against abuse. If a slave were hurt or killed, the criminal offense was against the slave owner for loss of property, not against the slave as a human being, but biblical laws assumed otherwise (Saggs, 1995: 56).

Biblical laws challenged debt slavery and slavery in general, and appear to be the first in the ancient world to declare such (Mendelsohn, 1949: 123; Weber, 1952: 64; Croatto, 1981 ; 36). Slaves were to be treated respectfully and to share in the family religious life: Sabbath (Exod 20:10; 23:12), sacrificial meals (Deut 12:12, 18; Lev 22:11), festivals (Deut 16:11, 14), and Passover (Exod 12:44). Slaves could rest on the Sabbath in Israel, but throughout the ancient world slaves would have worked continually, only the rich owners had leisure time (Wright, 1996: 76). In biblical laws slaves could be released contrary to the owner's desires. Slave release occurred if the master brutally beat the slave (Exod 21:20, 26–27). If the master beats a male or female slave, causing the slave to die, the owner could be punished (Exod 21:20). If the master struck the eye or knocked out a tooth of a male or female slave, the slave went free (Exod 21:26–27). In those primitive health conditions, it was very easy to knock out a tooth, thus encouraging a master not to hit the slave in the face altogether. Such protection could not be found elsewhere in the ancient world. Young slave girls were released, if they did not become full wives upon reaching adulthood (Exod 21:7–11). Most notable is the law demanding the death penalty for whomever kidnaps a person to sell him into slavery (Exod 21:6; Deut 24:7). A similar law demanding capital punishment for kidnapping, is in the Law Code of Hammurabi (Law #14), but it applied only to the young male children (minors) of free citizens of Babylon (Chilperic Edwards, 1904: 30). The Israelite law applied to all people. All of these protections appeared already in the Book of the Covenant.

Deuteronomy provides more radical guidelines; Deut 23:15–16 declares that a slave who escapes from a foreign country should not be returned to his land of origin, but should be allowed to live in the land of Israel wherever he wishes. Judahites thus violated universally recognized international laws regarding the return of escaped slaves across national borders (Loewenstamm, 1971: 252; Craigie, 1976: 300–1). Ancient Near Eastern fugitive slave laws were harsh on slave escape. Sumerian law in the third millennium and Nuzi laws in the late second millennium heavily fined someone who hid a fugitive slave. The Law Code of Hammurabi prescribed death for hiding or assisting an escaped slave (Roth, 1997: 84–5). Hittite laws from the Old Kingdom (1650–1500 BCE) mandate that the owners of an escaped slave reward those who bring back their slaves (Roth, 1997: 220). Also, the owner of a slave who had escaped could appeal to the state authorities to help him find and return that slave (Mendelsohn, 1947: 58–63). The contrasting biblical law in Deut 23:15–16 demonstrates the attitude of biblical authors toward slavery. The implementation of this guideline, if it were the practice of Judah under Josiah after 622 BCE, would have made Judah into a rogue state defying international law (Loewenstamm, 1971: 252; Craigie, 1976: 300–1). It was truly inspired by the memory that God save Israelites from slavery in Egypt, and this law particularly sows the seeds of modern abolitionism.

Debt Slave Release

Truly important legislation are those slave release laws which evolved throughout the history of the Israelite legal tradition. Exod 21:2–6 provides the earliest guidelines for debt slave release. Some scholars believe that with this law the biblical authors were really crafting ethical guidelines in the form of legal formulations (Arneth, 2013: 109–24). The law assumes that no debt is greater than six years of bonded service to a creditor. The text reads:

> (2) When you buy a Hebrew slave, he shall serve six years, and in the seventh he shall go out free, for nothing. (3)If he comes in single, he shall go out single; if he comes in married, then his wife shall go out with him. (4)If his master gives him a wife and she bears him sons or daughters, the wife and her children shall be her master's and he shall go out alone. (5) But if the slave plainly says, "I love my master, my wife, and my children; I will not go out free." (6) Then his master shall bring him to the door or the doorpost; and his master shall bore his ear through with an awl; and he shall serve him for life.

No provision for the release of female slaves occurs in this initial legal statement presumably she becomes the wife of her owner or is married to someone else (Lowery, 2000: 26). If the slave owner does not marry her, and no other spouse can be found, provision must be made for her redemption or release. The male slave may leave with his family, if they fell into slavery with him, but if the slave married and had children after becoming a slave, his family belonged to the master. Clever owners paired slave girls with their male debt slaves so that the resulting wedded couples with their children would stay permanently. The slave might say he loved his master, but probably male slaves loved their families and remained in slavery for their sake.

This debt slave release law could be circumvented by masters who "failed" to count the six years, and the male debt slave was forever in year four or five of his servitude. If the family of the male debt slave made legal appeal to the local village elders or to a more formally organized court in a larger walled city, they might discover that the judge was a relative of the affluent slave master or at least someone susceptible to a bribe. Clever slave masters could create a large number of permanent slaves.

Because of these loopholes, scribal legislators developed better protective laws for debt slaves. Deuteronomic Law promulgated Sabbath Year Release that combined debt release, which led to debt slavery, and better guidelines for debt slave emancipation. Selected verses in Deut 15:1–18 verses read:

> (1)At the end of every seven years you shall grant a release. (2)And this is the manner of the release, every creditor shall release what he has lent to his neighbor; he shall not exact it of his neighbor, his brother, because the Lord's release has been proclaimed. (3)Of a foreigner you may exact it; but whatever of yours is with your brother your hand shall release . . . (12)If your brother, a Hebrew man, or a Hebrew woman, is sold to you, he shall serve you six years, and in the seventh year you shall let him go free from you. (13)And when you let him go free from you, you shall not let him go empty-handed; (14)you shall furnish him liberally out of your flock, out of your threshing floor, and out of your wine press; as the Lord your God has blessed, you shall give to him.

The master is to act liberally in releasing the debt slave and thus to imitate God who releasing the slaves from bondage in Egypt. The rhetoric in this section makes the release of debt slaves a religious action (Houston, 2006: 186–8). Herein we observe social justice legislation undergirded vividly by the actions of a monotheistic deity.

There is perhaps a reference to the observance of this custom under Nehemiah around 444 BCE. The people of Judah promised, "we will forego the crops of the seventh year and the exaction of every debt" (Neh 10:31). Not growing crops on the seventh year refers to Fallow Year, a custom mentioned in Exod 23:10–11. If this release of debts is connected to Fallow Year, then the people may refer to the debt release law in Deut 15:1–2. This would indicate that the Sabbath Year debt release was taken seriously in the late fifth century BCE. Since a reference to debt slave release is lacking in Neh 10:31, this might explain why a reiteration of the customs were required by Leviticus 25, for Sabbath Year slave release was not being kept.

Allusions in texts imply an observance of Fallow Year land rest and Sabbath Year debt remission, for all the incidents fit in a seven-year chronological sequence. These include : (1) Jews exempted from taxes by Alexander the Great in 330 BCE; (2) loss of the fortress of Beth-Zur in 163-162 BCE by Judas Maccabeus due to Sabbath Year's lack of grain production (1 Macc 6:49–54); (3) failure of John Hyrcanus to avenge the death of Simon Maccabeus in 135–134 BCE due to Sabbath Year (Josephus); (4) Jerusalem taken by Herod and his general, Sossius, due to a food shortage caused by Sabbath Year in 37–36 BCE; (5) Seder Olam, a rabbinic tract, implies Jerusalem was destroyed after the Sabbath Year in 68–69 CE; (6) contracts at Murabba'at in Palestine in 132–133 CE imply the existence of a Sabbath Year; (7) Jewish tombstones refer to Sabbath Years in 433–434 CE and 440–441 CE; and (8) Tacitus recalls that Jews abstain from work every seventh year (North, 1954; de Vaux, 1961: 174; Wacholder, 1973: 158–84, 1976: 762–3; Pruitt, 2010: 81–92).

Debt release every seven years means the likelihood of poor people falling into debt slavery is greatly diminished. This Deuteronomic law especially attempts to prevent dishonest counting of years for an individual debt slave. Scholars suggest that the Deuteronomic law did this by a literary trick. The law of slave release in Deuteronomy 15 is connected to the law of debt release, a debt release that occurs every seven years throughout the land. The slave release law follows directly after the debt release law, giving the impression that a seven-year universal cycle is still assumed. Instead of a slave being released in the seventh year of his own personal servitude, now it appears that the debt slave is to be released at the same time that all debts are forgiven. The reference to the six years of debt slavery in verse 12 as a result becomes a reference to the fixed cycle of six years of national release mentioned in the previous passages concerning debt release (North, 1954: 33; Morgenstern, 1962: 4:142; Wacholder, 1976: 762–3). If all slaves were released at the same time, no dishonest counting could occur.

According to some authors, a universal release of all debt slaves would cause economic chaos (Phillips, 1970: 76–7, 1973: 106; Craigie, 1976: 238; Wright, 1996: 192–4; Leuchter, 2008: 637). But if you release debts you also release the debt slave, who no longer owes a debt, thus debts and debt slaves logically would be released at the same time (de Vaux, 1961: 173–4). The prophet Jeremiah alludes to slave release (Jer 34:8–11) in which all the debt slaves are released simultaneously, which is in accord with the Deuteronomic law. Reading the debt slave release law after the debt release law would naturally imply that debt slave release is on a seven-year national cycle like debt remission. This is a radical law articulated on behalf of slaves, even if it was not observed over the years (Leuchter, 2008: 641).

The legislation addresses women slaves, who now are also released in the seventh year of universal debt and slave release. They might have been the wives and daughters of householders who fell into deep financial distress, while the husbands and fathers of these women still retained their freedom. Or they might have been in debt slavery before their husbands and fathers fell into debt slavery, so they were not covered when the man fulfilled his six years of servitude. Perhaps, their husbands or fathers died in debt slavery. At any rate, they were not previously covered by the laws in Exodus 21, and now Deuteronomy 15 addresses their situation.

The slave master also must give provisions to the newly freed male slave, so that he will not fall back quickly into debt and debt slavery. Previously a slave master might have extended a loan immediately to a former debt slave knowing that the ex-debt slave soon would be his once more. Deuteronomic laws developed debt slave legislation in light of the previous two centuries of economic development and social abuse. This legislation is truly a humanitarian move to reform society and promote social justice (Nicholson, 1991: 191–204).

The Radical Law of Jubilee Year

Jubilee Year, a custom proclaimed in Leviticus 25, is the most dramatic legislation for the poor. Every forty-nine or fifty years the land was restored to the original family that owned it, so if a family fell into debt slavery and lost their farm, this law provided for the return of their land. This custom seeks to be even more humanitarian than earlier laws with the addition of land restoration (Jeffry Stackert, 2011: 242–3, 239–50).

This law may be inspired by the Mesopotamian customs of debt and slave release proclaimed by kings, but its regular implementation means it is not tied to the whim of a strong monarch who can initiate it (Milgrom, 1993: 8, 54; Weinfeld, 1995: 152–78; Hudson, 1999: 26–33, 44). Jews probably never practiced this custom, but it remained a vision of hope for poor people. This law builds upon the customs of Fallow Year and Sabbath Year, a seven-year cycle, and calls Jubilee Year as a cycle of seven cycles of seven years. Guidelines for land rest, the old Fallow Year, already mentioned in Exodus, are found in Lev 25:2–7, wherein the land is not to be cultivated but the volunteer crop from the previous year may be eaten by the owners, their servants, and the animals.

Jubilee Year follows after the seventh seven-year land rest. The author of Leviticus 25 wishes to retain the old custom of Fallow Year because of the food provisions for the poor and for slaves.

Debt slave release and land restoration guidelines are in Lev 25:39–55, and selected passages read as follows in verses 10, 39–41:

> (10)"And you shall hallow the fiftieth year and you shall proclaim liberty throughout the land to all its inhabitants. It shall be a jubilee for you: you shall return, every one of you, to your property and every one of you to your family. . . . (39)If any who are dependent on you become so impoverished that they sell themselves to you, you shall not make them serve as slaves. (40) They shall remain with you as hired or bound laborers. They shall serve with you until the year of the Jubilee. (41)Then they and their children with them shall be free from your authority ; they shall go back to their own family and return to their ancestral property."

Debt slaves, and particularly children who would have been born while their parents were debt slaves, come out of servitude. This law again seeks to end the practice of matchmaking by masters who sought to tempt their debt slaves into permanent slavery.

Perhaps, the Deuteronomic Sabbath year was not being kept, so the Priestly legislators crafted a variation on slave release, combining ideas from laws in the Book of the Covenant and the Deuteronomic Code. Some scholars believe that Sabbath Year was observed, but Jubilee was too idealistic to be implemented, especially since the forty-ninth and the fiftieth years would have been two consecutive land fallow years (de Vaux, 1961: 176–7; Fager, 1987: 59–68; Amit, 1992: 53–56). Other scholars think all the slave release laws were simply idealistic suggestions by biblical authors and never kept.

The idea of a forty-ninth and fiftieth years both releasing slaves does not sound realistic (Lowery, 2000: 57–77; Leuchter, 2008: 638–40). I have summarized the debate on the historicity of the custom (Gnuse, 1985: 43–8). Nonetheless, it has been called the most visionary and vigorous attempt in the laws of Israel in its attempt to ameliorate the woes of the poor peasants (Brueggeman, 1992: 80).

I believe Leviticus 25 proclaims an incredible vision of hope for poor, reminding the rich that someday the poor would stand beside them as equals in the community. Land restoration would still be a radical form of economic revival today.

Jubilee imperatives thus surpass the Book of the Covenant and Deuteronomic Laws by including land restoration. If former debt slaves can be resettled upon their original land, their economic future is more substantial than the provisions mandated by Deuteronomy 15, which may have been seen as insufficient by the author of Leviticus 25. But since this drastic measure may threaten the greater economic security of society, land restoration cannot come every seven years (Mitchell, 1912: 263; North, 1954: 135, 153; Porter, 1976: 205).For the longer period of time proposed for Jubilee Year, Leviticus laws provided rhetoric calling for better treatment of debt slaves. Lev 25:42–43, 46 demands that debt slaves not be treated harshly. Israelite debt slaves in Leviticus 25 are treated more generously than foreign slaves (Lev 25:44–46a), if there were any. But the biblical tradition will address this issue in later years, when the dignity of all slaves will be respected. Leviticus 25 may have laid the foundation for the Western European development of universal human abolitionism (Lowery, 2000: 70).

The evolving laws, culminating with Jubilee Year, sought to eliminate the oppression of debt slavery with expanded and drastic legislation to restore the slave's freedom and to give opportunity for financial independence. Biblical authors did not understand economics as we do, but they knew a society needs to maintain a healthy middle class or peasant class capable of production and contribution to the society.

Jubilee Year was a priestly utopian vision of hope designed to prevent the rich from garnering wealth at the expense of the poor in the struggling post-exilic and to prevent serious economic injustice. Jubilee laws espouse an egalitarian vision of humanity and a high view of the family unit as the cornerstone of society. The land is not an economic commodity but a gift from God to enable people to live honorably on the land free from poverty and oppression. It is a lesson worth heeding in most parts of our world today.

This moral vision of hope would inspire post-exilic prophets, the New Testament, and the later Jewish and Christian traditions in an ongoing evolutionary trajectory (Fager, 1987: 59–68; Amit, 1992: 47–59; Gerstenberger, 2007: 16–21; Carmichael, 2000: 509–25).

Additional Laws for the Poor

There are other laws in the legal corpora of the Old Testament that did not undergo a developmental trajectory as the ones just discussed, but they are worthy of mention for the goal of bringing justice for the poor. These were laws designed to prevent poor people from falling into poverty and being forced to take out loans and ultimately become debt slaves. We know not how faithfully these laws were observed, but at least, they were crafted by scribal theologians with a vision of how society should function.

Fallow Year guidelines are found in Exod 23:10–11, wherein fields lie fallow every seventh year so that "volunteer crops," or seeding from the previous year's harvest, may provide food for the poor and the animals. How did Fallow Year work?

Were all fields nation-wide left fallow for a year? Probably not! The law may have applied to individual fields on a rotating basis, and the land parcels may have been left fallow only for one growing season, either the fall or the spring crop, but not both seasons (Hopkins, 1985: 192–202). What is important about this legislation is that the poor people have access to the "volunteer crop."

Deut 14:28–29 speaks of a poor person's tithe for the Levites and the poor people of the land, the resident aliens, the widows, and the orphans. We have no evidence in the biblical text that this custom was ever undertaken. Nevertheless, we observe that this tithe every third year is to go to poor people in general and not to the Temple in Jerusalem.

Deut 24:14–15 and Lev 19:13, which is also found in the Code of Manu of India, require that employees who use day laborers, both Israelite and foreign, must pay these workers at the end of each day, so that they have food for their families. The workers would be those helping with harvest in either the spring or fall growing seasons. These workers are to be paid in grain or produce, and their wages would be used immediately as food for their poor families. The law prevents employees from short-changing the workers, for if a worker was paid at the end of the week, the employer could claim that the worker only worked four days when he actually was present for six days. Such shortchanging often occurs even today. This law provides for fair payment and prevents exceptionally poor people from failing into debt slavery.

Many widows existed due to war and because women married older men. Gleaning customs helped widows, as well as other poor people. The poor were allowed to follow behind the reapers and bundlers of the grain and pick up fragments left behind, so that they could make bread for their families. Deut 23:19–21 adds an extra benefit for the poor by saying that if an entire sheaf is left behind in the field, the mistake benefits the poor. Furthermore, with high yield cash crops like grapes and olives, one should deliberately leave some of the produce behind for the poor on the vines. Lev 19:9–10 and 23:22 have a parallel demand that gleaners should not reap to the edges of the field in addition to leaving the gleanings so that the poor may gather this produce. In the subsistence economy of the ancient world, all farmers struggled to stay alive. Leaving something behind in the field was truly a sacrifice. How were these guidelines enforced? We do not know. This is truly preaching rhetoric inspired by faith in Yahweh. We today should be inspired by these texts, for we are part of an evolving trajectory created by these texts and we continue the process of bringing justice for the poor and the dispossessed of our world.

The Inspiration of Laws

The laws in Deuteronomy 12–26 particularly expanded upon the laws in Exodus 21–23 and the laws in Leviticus continue to address some of the same issues. The laws sought rights for poor people who had been disadvantaged by economic and political development in the eighth and seventh centuries BCE by rich and powerful people. The authors of Deuteronomy 12–26 were inspired by eighth-century BCE prophets, and the themes in their new laws were the exclusive worship of one God and the defense of the poor and marginal elements of society. Monotheism or the exclusive worship of one God and social justice spearheaded the rhetoric of the entire book of Deuteronomy in a closely intertwined fashion. With the cry for the exclusive worship of Yahweh there appeared a cry for justice and an attempt to legislate guidelines for the poor and marginal people. Deuteronomic Laws unfold latent ideas found in the earlier laws of the Book of the Covenant, but their fuller manifestation came only in the later evolution of human experience. The cultural and historical experience of Israel developed the concepts of exclusive worship of Yahweh and social reform in the years prior to the exile, and in post-exilic literature we see further development in some of the Priestly texts in Leviticus (Albertz, 1994b: 1:1–242). The implications of these religious, social, and legal insights would continue to unfold in the Christian movement.

4 The Relationship of Monotheism to Social Justice
New Scholarly Paradigms

Scholars now stress the gradual nature of Israel's religious development and their religious and cultural continuity with the ancient world. Monotheism arose out of a complex evolving matrix of beliefs observable in ancient texts for millennia before Israel was born. With the sixth-century BCE Babylonian Exile a large number of Judahites or Jews were ready to affirm monotheism, and subsequently the biblical literature as we would recognize it was generated. Exclusive devotion to Yahweh arose over six centuries of pre-exilic history and came to culmination in the exilic, after which a cadre of faithful believers spread monotheism to the Jewish masses. We suggest they developed the ideas they inherited and laid the foundation for the values found in our western culture. As we now speak of gradual processes in Israel's history, how will this affect biblical theology?

The emergence of monotheism was not an inevitable process predestined to arise in the human cultural experience. Were it not for the Babylonian Exile, which threw a small number of Jewish intelligentsia into Mesopotamia where they had to reflect upon their understanding in Yahweh vis-á-vis the beliefs of polytheists all around them, monotheism would not have emerged among the Jews at all. We might be heirs to Hellenistic monism, such as is found in the teachings of the Greek thinker Xenophanes. In India, monotheistic notions were connected with deities such as Indra and Varuna, but they never captured the hearts of the masses. Instead, philosophical monism was the path chosen by Indian intellectuals. Monotheism emerges under rarified social conditions, such as exile. Believers must affirm their god against the gods of the land in order to affirm their identity and survive as a people. Toleration of those others deities will lead to some form of henotheism or a philosophical monism that accepts a plurality of personal deities while affirming one impersonal divine principle.

The exile of religious intelligentsia in a foreign land, pressured to forsake their ancestral beliefs, may be the prerequisite to the development of radical monotheism.

V. Nikiprowetsky testifies that specific historical and cultural phenomena are required for pure monotheism to emerge:

> It must be realized that ethical monotheism was not a 'natural' and universal fait accompli, destined for all mankind from the very beginning.... It simply represents the culmination of a historical process belonging to Israel and to Israel alone.... If, then, monotheism required centuries to reach maturity, ... we cannot stress too much how slowly this process evolved in practice.... it does represent a true spiritual revolution and it continues to deserve being

considered as one of the moral and intellectual bases of modern society.
(Nikiprowetsky, 1975: 69, 80, 86)

Exclusive devotion to one deity may emerge in evolutionary fashion in the
preliminary stages, but the emergence of monotheism is more of a revolutionary
breakthrough. This author also believes that the emergence of monotheism is an
unfinished process, especially in regard to the social justice that it engenders.
Ideas latent in the early stages of monotheistic emergence may take centuries to
come to full fruition, such as the abolition of slavery and the equality of women.
Monotheism in its fullest form has been emerging for 3,000 years, and we are
still part of that evolution and revolution.

We now envision Israelites gradually emerging out of Canaanite and ancient
Near Eastern culture with significant differences arising in the Babylonian Exile
and beyond. But sixty and fifty years ago, when I was a student, biblical
theologians declared that Israelites, early in their history, created a worldview
with a sense of equality and justice. They declared that this ethos stood in
diametric opposition to ancient Near Eastern beliefs and practices. Some of
them declared this Israelite ethos emerged already in revolutionary fashion with
Moses or in the early settlement period around 1200 BCE.

We were urged to heed the message of the biblical text and become advocates
of justice, thus repeating the great monotheistic and social breakthrough accomplished so long ago by ancient Israel. We were called upon to oppose consump-
tion, greed, and disregard for marginal people in the modern world. Biblical
theologians contrasted Israelite and Canaanite values to parallel contemporary
biblically inspired social values against the oppressive and narcissistic values in
our modern American and European society. As our biblical predecessors
struggled against oppressors back then, faithful Jews and Christians were to
continue the struggle in modern times. The rhetoric was inspiring and quite apt
for our modern age, but it extremely stereotyped the ancient world and Israel.

Early Israel was seen as a democratic and monotheistic society under Moses
and Joshua, but those values were supposedly compromised by later kings,
especially Solomon. Solomon's supposed return to the old city-state system
made his social agenda sound strikingly similar to modern capitalistic society,
and the monotheistic and egalitarian values of the prophets and Deuteronomic
reform movements, which opposed revisionist kings, contained the elements
that liberal Jewish and Christian social reformers and theologians espoused in
the modern age.

In that age, from 1950 to 1980, theologians and biblical scholars communi-
cated this message to seminarians, preachers, and leading lay intellectuals. One
notable example were the writing efforts of Walter Brueggemann, who still

proclaims a message of social justice today (Brueggemann, 1978: 9–113, 1992: 1–307; and especially, 1995: 27–51). I, too, wrote in a similar vein. We had a haunting awareness that ours may not have been an objective portrayal of the scholarly issues and themes in the biblical text, but this message made the biblical text relevant, and the social message for the modern era is still meaningful today. But with our newer understanding of the Israelite settlement process and the later and more gradual emergence of monotheism, our old teaching paradigms and textbooks are uncomfortably dated. We need to understand in a new way how monotheistic thought arose in the intellectual matrix of those ancient Jews. We also need to craft a new theological message for ourselves with the conviction found in the theological expressions of a previous age. Simply because the biblical and scholarly paradigms have changed, there is no reason to lose the message of social justice and human equality.

How Monotheism Changes the Worldview

Even though the stark contrast between Israel and the ancient Near East was in error, there was some truth in our theological conclusions. As monotheism gradually emerged, it germinated new social and religious insights. Though many of those beliefs can be found in contemporary ancient Near Eastern texts, it might be said that Israel simply moved further along the trajectory of evolution. If formerly we said that Israel viewed Yahweh as a god of history while ancient Near Easterners saw their deities as merely nature deities, now we would say that everyone viewed their gods as social deities acting on the "historical plain," but biblical texts stressed this dimension more.

Monotheism emerged with a new synthesis of old ideas, often raising to a higher level certain concepts and values previously held in subordinate fashion in the ancient Near Eastern agenda. This new worldview was "neither wholly discontinuous nor ... a random collection of features from older versions" of cosmic and social visions of reality (Hendel, 1992: 17). In the old worldview we find perceptions of Mesopotamian gods (Ashur and Marduk) who act in history, notions of universalism (especially Atenism), ethics, and a demand for social justice in the literatures of Egypt and Mesopotamia (especially wisdom literature), but post-exilic biblical literature moved forward in a new synthesis of monotheistic belief. Though biblical thought is not unique, biblical authors go beyond their predecessors in reconfiguring ideas. This synthesis creates something new, even though specific elements of the worldview are old, as once previously recessive ideas become dominant in the new monotheistic faith.

The destruction of Judah in 586 BCE and the concomitant collapse of their political and ideational world-view demanded a re-articulation of their beliefs.

They had less respect for the old traditions of the greater ancient Near East, especially as a landless people who no longer could view their deity as a god of their "land." Some of these ideas existed among their intelligentsia prior to exile. Israelites and Jews were a "peripheral society," outside the great river valley cultures of Egypt and Mesopotamia, they were selective in choosing the language, ideas, and customs from those high cultures. Their self-portrayal as escaped slaves, which was not really true, nonetheless made them less respectful of received values. Thus, they disdained the divine status of kings (Gnuse, 2011), the use of nature imagery to envision their God, and an iconic portrayal of God. The latter gave too much power to kings and priests who made and controlled the images. With emerging monotheism they removed multiple wills in the divine real and reduced the multiplicity of forms in understanding the divine.

Deuteronomic Reform before the exile developed the image of covenant as a metaphor to describe their relationship to God. God was metaphored as a king, a social image, in place of the old storm god imagery. This anthropomorphic imagery of the Deuteronomists contrasted with nature imagery still used along with social images in the rest of the ancient Near East. The new Deuteronomic covenant-oriented religion moved in a more social and humanistic direction, stressing ethical norms and the value of the individual (Geller, 2000: 273–319; Halpern, 1991: 77–91). After the exile this ideology continued to minds of people over the next few centuries, especially with the newly crafted biblical texts. How the texts were used to affect broad public understandings, we do not know.

Sixty years ago biblical theologians said Yahwism developed morality and ethics, while ancient Near Eastern religions contained only cultic activity with no moral norms.

This overlooked the literary tradition represented by the Egyptian wisdom tradition in the collections of sayings in Ptah-hotep (2500 BCE), Amen-em-het (1900 BCE), Amen-emope (1100 BCE), and in stories like the Tale of the Eloquent Peasant (2100 BCE). Moral values are found in texts which call upon the Mesopotamian kings to engage in moral social behavior and to uphold justice in the land, especially for the poor. Critical scholars even noted this in those years (Hammershaimb, 1960: 75–101; Fensham, 1962: 161–71; Malchow, 1966: 1–6). Moshe Weinfeld in later years undertook an extensive evaluation of how notions of justice for the oppressed are found throughout both the ancient Near East and Israel (Weinfeld, 1995). It was wrong for us to speak of the ancient Near East as lacking morality and ethical standards, especially when we knew better at the time.

However, we can ask whether such social and ethical literature in Egypt and Mesopotamia had any significant impact upon everyday society (Dever, 2000: 62–7). Was it merely the property of intellectuals and the scribal elite? Could such literature have made an impact upon the fixed authoritarian societies of Egypt and Mesopotamia?

It appears that Jews in the post exilic era used the social guidelines of the Deuteronomic tradition of the biblical text more effectively in shaping their society than we observe elsewhere. Jews may have been capable of this, because they lived in a simpler society than the river cultures of Egypt and Mesopotamia, and the social pressure to maintain the old cultural institutions was not as great. With a wider use of the alphabet, a higher degree of literacy meant that a larger number of people were intelligentsia, and in postexilic Judah this might mean that more intellectuals familiar with the biblical texts might help shape their society by these new norms. However, we simply do not know how this process might have occurred after 500 BCE in Judah.

Since Israel and post-exilic Judah stood on the periphery of the high cultures, they could "appropriate" and modify ideas from the river valley cultures. Similarly, Phoenicians invented the alphabet when strong scribal guides in Egypt and Mesopotamia prevented its emergence a thousand years earlier so that they could retain their scribal positions, which took years of study to attain. Greece, another peripheral society, made strides in government, philosophy, and law, all inspired by ideas from Mesopotamia and Egypt.

Perhaps, post-exilic Jews emphasized ethics more than the preceding cultures. In a polytheistic or henotheistic worldview there are many gods with conflicting divine wills, as cosmogonic myths such as the Atrahasis Epic and the Enuma Elish imply (Saggs, 1995: 116). In Genesis 1 the world is generated and ordered by one deity without such conflict. In monotheism one deity absorbs the functions of the other gods. Yahweh became supreme over all the forces of nature, rendering these forces no longer divine.

One will permeates the universe; divine conflict is gone. The conflict of divine wills in Mesopotamian myths now was replaced by one divine will directing the universe without conflict or challenge (Frymer-Kensky, 1992: 83–99). This is also true in monistic systems where one divine impersonal will swallows up the gods. But then believers often equate that divine presence with all of nature. In monotheism devotees view that singular personal deity as being beyond the natural realm, though ruling it.

The conflict of divine wills found in polytheistic worldviews may affect moral values. The polytheistic world is divided among the various gods, each requiring veneration. These many superhuman wills fail to provide a single moral imperative to people; different deities require diverse moral and cultic responses. A monotheistic divine will above gives clear moral imperatives to people below, and this can entail a commission to provide social justice in society. Though polytheists have ethical imperatives, they know not whether a particular ethical mandate represents the will of all the gods. With such diversity, no assurance exists that their particular moral conduct will please the divine realm, so they must resort to prayers and sacrifices to appease the different deities. Clear ethical imperatives from one divine will offer certitude for faithful believers. The demands of diverse divine wills in the heavens are ended, and subsequently believers can respond to a deity with assurance, and direct their prayer without using sacrifice as a persuasive device to obtain the deity's attention (as in the prayers of the post-exilic Psalter)(Moltmann, 1985: 51–2; Frymer-Kensky, 1992: 15, 116; van Beeck, 1992: 225–6; Albertz, 1994a: 81; Dever, 2000: 65; Geller, 2000: 312–5).

Polytheisms with many gods do not make clear moral and social demands upon people, due to the multiplicity of wills in the divine realm. With one God there is a greater likelihood that the one deity will make a wider range of demands upon believers, and these will include moral and social norms. The "immense God" of a monotheistic faith asks much of the believers and receives it (Stark, 2013: 324–5). As Yahweh leads Israel out of Egypt, Yahweh demonstrates total power over the gods of the Egyptians in the plagues and the sea crossing. Yahweh alone is God and demonstrates justice in liberating the slaves. Then the slaves are led to Sinai where they receive the Law, which in the final written form of the biblical text spans Exodus and Leviticus (Bills, 2020: 171–254). This is an "immense" moral imperative from an "immense" singular God. Thus, "monotheism has great capacities to mobilize human actions – capacities far beyond those found in polytheisms or in Godless religion" (Stark, 2013: 11). The eventual emergence of monotheism corresponds with increasing morality in the "law" codes that emphasizes human equality. It takes time, but eventually that "legal morality" will have influence upon the society in which the religion flourishes. Numerous scholars have traced the powerful social justice imperatives that permeate the biblical text (Weinfeld, 1995; Epsztein, 1986; Pleins, 2001; Nardoni, 2004).

Monotheistic and polytheistic literary texts may appear similar, but the morality is found in the greater message of the total biblical text. The difference between the Mesopotamian and biblical flood accounts, for example, is not in differences of narrative detail but in the overall monotheism of the biblical narrative with its divine control and moral purpose. The flood comes about because of human sin, not noise generated by people that disturbs the gods or a rebelliousness in serving the gods. The biblical text has God talk directly to Noah, close the ark door (I guess Noah forgot to attach the doorknob), steady the boat in the water (God has wellies), and bring the ark to rest on the mountain in Ararat. In the Mesopotamian accounts Enki must speak to the house or the wall of the flood hero, lest he lose his divine status for divulging the coming flood to a human being. The gods are affrighted by the rising flood waters (Ishtar screamed by a woman in labor), and they subsequently argue with Enki when they discover people have survived. Monotheism changes the whole dynamic of the story's meaning (Finkelstein, 1958: 440–3).

Monotheism also puts a greater value and responsibility upon people with these increased moral demands. Not only are people commissioned to a higher level of moral behavior, they are imbued with a greater sense of the divine in human nature.

With so many gods of the pantheon gone, some of the activities attributed to deities now become attributed to humanity. For example, in Genesis 4 the invention of certain human functions, such as farming, shepherding, city-building, metal work, musical instruments, and other comparable functions are attributed to people like Cain, Jubal, Tubal-Cain, and others. A polytheistic worldview attributes these inventions to the gods, as in Mesopotamia, but in Israel they are human inventions, accomplished with divine blessing, but human in origin, nonetheless (Frymer-Kensky, 1992: 108–17). The old gods have disappeared, replaced by humans. Randall Garr has creatively interpreted Gen 1:26 in this regard. When God says, "let us" make people in our image, God is speaking to other divine beings. Their passive consent to the decision to create people in the divine image is the victory of monotheism over the other gods. They have been supplanted by people as divine agents in the cosmos. People in the "divine image" replace those other gods or divine beings, who now disappear in the Priestly narrative (later references to God saying "let us" appear in the Yahwist narrative (Garr, 2003: 201–5). Furthermore in Psalm 8 people are said to be raised to a nearly divine status now that the heavens have been emptied of the other gods. Psalm 8 contains a paraphrase of Gen 1:26 especially with the "rulership mandate" (Garr, 2003: 220–2). "God demotes the gods" and humanity replaces them, for "without gods, there is a vacuum in God's world" and God "loses an entire administrative stratum" in the "governance of the world" that must be replaced by human beings (Garr, 2003: 222). Garr's language is colorful but very appropriate. The emergence of monotheism brings an elevation in the value of people.

Monotheism and Morality

With the disappearance of the gods and the ascendancy of one god, people have more freedom. Monotheism proclaims the freedom of the deity in the divine realm to act without the constraints of the other divine wills. If God is free, then all actions in the cosmos are free. This then affirms human freedom, and their actions in the social arena are more important. There is equality of people in the human realm as believers relate equally to that one deity. As that God is free in the divine realm, correspondingly the devotees are free in the earthly realm.

One clear divine will communicates to people in revelation, and then human beings become responsible for what occurs in this realm. Social disaster does not happen by fate or capricious accident, it happens because of human activity. What occurs in the world is not due to a divine will other than God's, but it must be in response to human actions or behavior, for there is only one divine will in the divine realm. People are more responsible for their fate, because God is responding to them.

With this radical sense of human accountability, exclusive monotheism puts the burden of the world and human existence more in human hands than polytheism with its tension of divine powers. Repeatedly in the biblical law codes and the prophets we see the text declare that if people do not help the poor in their midst, God will act dramatically to help the poor and even punish those who failed to heed the cry of the poor (Kaiser, 1972: 70). One deity in the divine realm would take on such a responsibility, but one deity among a host of deities would not act so boldly.

The creation accounts in both Israel and Mesopotamia describe the careful creation of humanity from the ground. But in Mesopotamia humans are made from the blood of an evil god, be it We-ilu in the Atrahasis Epic or Kingu in the Enuma Elish, and the people are destined to serve the gods as slaves and perform a ritual function to support the gods and correspondingly the kings and priests. In Israel they are made from the breath of the good God and serve as free moral agents who share responsibility with God for the stewardship of the universe (Alter, 1981: 28–30). People are responsible and accountable for their actions. Because people are thus accountable for their actions, the religious tradition generates ethical imperatives, commands to do those things which will please the deity.

Ethical imperatives challenge humanity more deeply, leading to a sense of human finitude, personal guilt, and inadequacy. Believers are prone to speak more of human guilt rather than impurity and of the need for forgiveness more than purification.

There are now verbal moral imperatives that ultimately can be read from a written text.

Orally proclaimed moral messages first emerge with the pre-exilic prophets and are subsequently converted into written literature in the exilic and post-exilic eras. This authoritative written literature ultimately replaces statuary and iconography. One deity existing in the divine realm can no longer be imagined by one of the many metaphors of nature, so thus revelation can be found only in the spoken or written word. Symbolic metaphors replace the more physical and material images (often statuary) of the old cult. A divine "word" replaces a divine "image" and the ethical imperatives are clearer, resulting in a greater emphasis upon social behavior rather than cultic actions.

Furthermore, the social behavior is incumbent upon all adherents to the faith, whereas the cultic actions were undertaken only by the specialized cultic personnel. This new biblical ethic imperative carries power and authority not because of the specific content of moral imperatives, but because of the powerful address to human existence from a distant and singular deity. The listener now has a greater responsibility to respond and obey, and this leads to a greater awareness of human freedom and responsibility.

Jewish ethics may not differ in content from the ancient Near Eastern texts, but there is a change in the understanding of the context in which they are expressed (Finkelstein, 1958: 438–42; Moriarity, 1974: 345–62; Moyer, 1983: 19–38; Theissen, 1985: 75; Elkana, 1986: 53; Halpern, 1991: 77–91; Otto, 1994: 215–9).

Monotheism is prone to emphasize the equality of human beings more than polytheism. Polytheistic systems with a multitude of gods have a class system for the gods. There are high gods who rule the significant phenomena of our world, there are major deities beneath them who are in charge of lesser functions, and then there are the smaller deities who specialize in distinctive functions (god of dreams, patron deities of various human professions, gods who answer specialized petitions, etc.). There are high gods and the lesser divinities ranked by importance and according to their function in the natural order (gods of the sky, sun, and storm are usually supreme). Lesser deities serve in the court of those high deities This class system in the heavens is mirrored on earth in the class system of: (1) rulers, priests, and warriors; (2) craftsmen, merchants, scribes, and other professionals; and finally (3) laborers and peasants, who constitute 90 percent of the population. On earth you have the elite leaders and the rest of the members of society who serve them. With the elimination of a class system in the heavens, one will unconsciously lessen the importance of the class system on earth. One deity in the divine realm undercuts the privilege of elites and subordinates on earth by removing those distinctions in the divine realm. When the tiered class system of the gods in the heavens disappears, the tiered class system of people on earth disappears (Handy, 1994; Gnuse 1997: 242–63).

There is one single universal basis for religious belief and human morality in monotheism, which in turn becomes a standard for all men and women to adhere to regardless of class or status. This further promotes equality of all believers before one deity and one unified natural order of things (Dever, 2000: 62–67). Egalitarian values then surface in the literature that is produced (Alter, 1981: 129).

One can observe such values in both the Old Testament and the New Testament. If there is one god in the heavens, then all people will relate to him equally. The idea that all believers stand before God as equals, at least in theory, is a cardinal assumption in all the monotheistic faiths. Though it may take 2,000 years for democracy to arise, the monotheistic beliefs will set the process in motion. It may be retarded by rulers and conquerors who use the religion to justify their imperial ambitions, but eventually the monotheistic urge to egalitarians will make itself felt in the social values. Revolutions take time.

This view of human freedom and responsibility was deepened by the newly developing view of the universe. Jews saw the cosmos less from a vantage point of timelessness ("cosmic time") and fated-ness because of the affirmation that the people of God originated at a point in time (Abraham or the exodus) and not at the beginning of the universe. The people in Genesis 1–3 were ancestors of all humanity, but Israel's ancestors come much later in time. The universe was more "unpredictable," not determined so much by fate. Whereas polytheists tried to discern the "predictable" in the conflict of the divine wills, Jewish thinkers accepted unpredictability that results when one god gives decrees that turn the potential for decision making over to people.

This singular deity then wills them to do good. Sin is not rebellion against cosmic harmony or cosmic fates, but against this singular divine will. The imagery of covenant becomes much more important, as people relate directly to one God, a personal being and not cosmic fate. For polytheists the gods are windows to the absolute, but for monotheists God is the absolute. Because believers have a direct relationship to that one God, the impersonal universe with its image of fated-ness surrenders to a theistic universe that mandates humans to action, especially moral actions in the social realm (Bucellati, 1995: 3:1685–96).

The needs of the poor and the oppressed were addressed by ancient Near Eastern texts, but the biblical tradition may have achieved a significant advance over the rhetoric of previous cultures. Egyptian and Mesopotamian texts which spoke on behalf of the poor came from middle class scribes, or intelligentsia, who did not rule. Texts grandly proclaiming that the king or pharaoh was responsible for justice were simply political propaganda. Mesopotamian law codes recognized class identity in the process of administering justice, so that a poor person is liable for a greater punishment for a crime that a rich person might also commit. Laws protected people of power and wealth against the poor. But the Jews wrote down the dissident words of prophets and the reform oriented laws, discussed in earlier sections, which were proclaimed as a religious and social guide for the reconstruction of the post-exilic community of Judaism. No other society elevated the literature of dissent seriously enough to convert it into a sacred text. This is a significant observation to make.

Rhetoric to care for the poor, the widow, and the orphan is found in other ancient texts, but the Jews made this message more central in their laws. They connected it to the central message of Jewish faith, the deliverance from Egypt by Yahweh. The message of monotheism and social justice was intertwined. The appeal for a just society is connected integrally to the image of Yahweh as the liberator of slaves.

While gods of the ancient Near East were portrayed primarily as world creators, the biblical texts stressed how Yahweh freed slaves. Biblical authors emphasized the historical and social dimension more than the cosmic dimension. This proclamation of how Yahweh liberated slaves provides immanence to the deity and balances the image of transcendence resulting from being the only god in the heavens (Moltmann, 1985: 51–2; Sperling, 1986: 22; Uffenheimer, 1986: 144; Luckert, 1991: 128). Emerging monotheism was connected to the struggle for justice and social equality, and this arose even more after the destruction of Jerusalem and their homeland in 586 BCE, when the intelligentsia were free to articulate these values for the creation of a new society (Lohfink, 1983: 28–47, 1985: 25; Albertz, 1994b: 1:63–65; Stolz, 1994: 184). The dramatic portrayal of Yahweh as the liberator deity of slaves and the call for a just society distinguished the biblical tradition from other predecessor cultures. The passion in the biblical text, the many laws, and the prophetic cry for reform indicate that the biblical tradition moved beyond the ancient world in its cry for justice and equality and devotion to a singular deity.

Judaism may have been the first true monotheism (with the debate on Zoroastrianism so uncertain), and it prepared for the later monotheisms of Christianity and Islam. It is crucially significant that the core event is the proclamation of Yahweh as the liberator of slaves. This elevates not only the social dimension, but it provides sympathy for the oppressed and lowly, an imperative for a just society, and the message that all people were radically equal before God.

Modern Relevance

How do these new understandings enable us to weave a message of inspiration for our church and classroom audiences so that we can call for social reform and justice in our world today? Monotheism and egalitarian social values did not arise early in Israel's history, but they did arise gradually in the exilic and post-exilic eras. Religious and social beliefs intertwined in monotheism have become foundational for Jews and Christians today.

If believers sense the presence of God in the social and historical dynamics of the odyssey to monotheism and social justice in the first millennia BCE, then they should sense a divine presence in the modern cultural process. Seeing God in the on-going process of developing monotheism today is more intellectually honest than the old model of dialectical contrast between Israel and the ancient world, or the between the modern Christian and world culture today. To perceive that monotheism arose over many years may enable us to understand that we are still on the trajectory of continuing religious and social change.

The Jewish and Christian traditions, twin branches of the monotheistic faith of Israel, have moved forward over the centuries in somewhat irregular fashion. Both have become encumbered with their own institutional agenda, the appeasement of political forces, and the preservation of stability in the synagogue/church. Theological leaders must reach deep into the biblical tradition to recall for us the imperative for social justice. In the history of Christendom we have vacillated back and forth between institutional stability and brief dynamic eras of reform (Käsemann, 1964: 63–94). The proclamation of modern prophetic-like theologians to the spirit of the biblical faith must affirm the on-going religious and intellectual tradition of monotheism rooted in the Bible. We must proclaim the equality of all people, advocate for the rights of women, minorities, immigrants, the poor, and people of different sexual persuasions.

We can acknowledge that some of the values found in the scriptures are less moral than what we believe today. We must recognize the evolutionary trajectory in religious belief and ethics initiated by the biblical tradition, then we will be able to concede that there are aspects of the biblical tradition which are primitive and must be discarded by us (slavery, holy war, patriarchalism, etc.). Our rejection of some of these ancient messages, however, abides by the very spirit of that biblical tradition. We should be faithful to the spirit, not the letter of the biblical text.

Biblical texts were a religious and intellectual breakthrough for the first millennium BCE, but in contrast to the very idealistic assumptions of our modern age, many of those values appear primitive. Morton Smith and Joseph Hoffman have shown this in a volume of essays (Smith and Hoffman, 1989: 11–237). This volume unveils the primitive state of ethical beliefs and practice taught by biblical authors. But biblical texts arose two millennia ago, and our religious beliefs and ethical sensitivities exist today because they have been inspired by those very texts. The biblical tradition began a long developmental process that would transcend many of its own cultural assumptions. We cannot enslave ourselves to the literal values of the biblical text with a stringent doctrine of biblical authority. The Bible does not create a set of values from which we cannot change or develop.

We must tap the roots of contemporary scholarship to discover new ways of thinking and speaking. We, too, should acknowledge that we are imperfect as we evolve toward a fuller monotheistic faith. Monotheism did not arise until late in Israel's history, likewise religious and social implications of monotheism have not yet unfolded totally in our own age. We do not seek to "return" to the biblical values literally, we endeavor to "develop" or "unfold" them as we move into the future.

This will help us face some of the issues we face in the text. Statements in the Hebrew Bible and the New Testament affirm the equality of all believers before God, but in women and children were subordinate to men, and slavery was a tolerated institution. Paul proclaims that in Christ there is neither Greek nor Jew, male nor female, slave nor free, yet in his letters he accepts slavery and the lower status of women in the Greco-Roman world. We must recognize that not all the implications of the Christian message could be implemented in his own age. But those very same teachings of Paul (as well as the Hebrew Bible before him) implied that someday slavery should be abolished and women be granted equality (Bauckham, 1987: 109).

Christianity drew forth the implications of the biblical message concerning the abolition of slavery and the elevation of women's rights within the past two centuries.

We can lament that it took centuries longer than it should have, but such was the fate of history. There is a necessary process of unfolding the total implications of great intellectual breakthroughs, such as monotheism. All the implications of the biblical message could not be worked out in terms of their social justice in one generation, especially since those early Christians were socially marginal and few in numbers in the tyrannical Roman Empire. But the process was begun, and it has been coming to fulfillment ever since. We are still part of that process. Richard Bauckham affirms:

> "Hence, in Israel, freedom entailed not inequality, but equality. That this principle of freedom was not carried through with complete consistency–in relation, for example, to the status of women, or to the institution of slavery . . . should not obscure the enormous significance of the breakthrough in principle." (Bauckham, 1987: 106)

At times Christians have understood this process. For example, the moral guidelines concerning the waging of holy war are understood as instructions given to the ancient Israelites, but not the later Christians, because the ethic of Jesus surpassed those militaristic injunctions. Christians have realized that the older biblical legislation had been given for an earlier people, but was not universally valid for all time. This, in part, is recognizes the historically conditioned nature of that legislation. Modern Jews and Christians stand back from the texts in Deuteronomy concerning holy war and recognize these passages should not be fulfilled literally today. We have evolved beyond their religious piety on many ethical issues, but we are still rooted in those ancient texts for the foundation of our modern piety.

However, there are aspects of the legal tradition in the Hebrew Bible which still speak to modern Christians, especially imperatives which deal with social justice.

Christians take the "spirit" of these laws and their rhetoric to call for justice for all people in our modern world. We reach back and use the old laws in a new way for our modern social and religious context (Otto, 1994: 18–116, 175–219. As Richard Bauckham observes:

> "Old Testament law can be a model for us not as a static blueprint, but as a dynamic process whose direction we can follow, in some cases, beyond the point at which the law itself had to stop" (Bauckham, 1987: 37).

We use these laws in our theology and preaching today because ultimately those Hebrew laws provide the foundation for our belief systems, even though we have advanced beyond some of them.

Though we can never return to the total belief system of the biblical text. Rather, we study those texts and by faith and insight intuit what messages have enduring relevance for us. We all know to some degree, conservatives and liberals, that our social situation is different from theirs, but where Christians disagree is the extent to which we modify the ancient biblical norms in the modern context. We all reinterpret the biblical text to some degree when we apply it to our modern situation. The call for justice and equality in today's society must still be inspired by the biblical tradition.

Final Observations

It took Christians 1,900 years to understand that the biblical testimony sought the abolition of slavery, and another century passed before the women received equality with men in both society and the church. Those and other values lay latent in the biblical text awaiting proclamation and had to lie dormant in the biblical text until society was capable of heeding their implications. The implications for a new worldview were present in early Israel down through the post-exilic era. But those early Israelites and post-exilic Jews could not have conceived of what would come from their beliefs. Social and religious values developed and significant insights surfaced with creative spokespersons, and the ideas crystallized in the minds of the average Jews, so that eventually monotheism became the worldview for many people.

The values of monotheism and social justice made their impact upon society in the past 500 years in western European Christian society. Perhaps, these ideas could not make their full impact until the biblical text was made available to a wider range of people, which was the result of Gutenberg's invention of the printing press and the dissemination of the Bible translated in the vernacular languages of various European cultures. If this is important in the emergence of these monotheistic values in the past 500 years, it might explain why egalitarian and democratic values emerged more readily in northern Europe and America. For it was there that Bible reading was highly prized. Reading the Bible is dangerous; it can inspire revolution.

References

Albertz, R. (1994a). Der Ort des Monotheismus in der israelitischen Religionsgeschichte, In W. Dietrich and M. Klopfenstein, eds., Ein Gott allein? JHWH-Verehrung und biblischer Monotheismus im Kontext der israelitischen und altorientalischen Religionsgeschichte OBO 139, Göttingen: Vandenhoeck & Ruprecht, pp. 77–96.

(1994b). A History of Israelite Religion in the Old Testament Period, 2 vols., trans. J. Bowden, OTL, Philadelphia, PA: Westminster.

Alter, R. (1981). The Art of Biblical Narrative, New York: Basic Books.

Amit, Y. (1992). The Jubilee Law – an Attempt at Instituting Social Justice. In G. Reventlow and Y. Hoffman, eds., Justice and Righteousness: Biblical Themes and their Influence, JSOTSup 137, Sheffield: JSOT Press, pp. 47–59.

Andersen, F., and Freedman, D. N. (1989). Amos, AB, New York: Doubleday.

Anderson, J. (2015). Monotheism and Yahweh's Appropriation of Baal, LHBOTS 617, London: Bloomsbury.

Arneth, M. (2013). Der Exodus der Sklaven. KD, 59, 109–24.

Assmann, J. (1997). Moses the Egyptian: The Memory of Egypt in Western Monotheism, Cambridge, MA: Harvard University Press.

Bauckham, R. (1987). The Bible in Politics, Louisville, KY: Westminster John Knox.

Van Beeck, F. J. (1992). Israel's God, the Psalms, and the City of Jerusalem. Hor, 19, 219–39.

De Benoist, A. (1981). Comment peut-on être païen?, Paris: n.p.

(1997). Vu de droite, Paris: n.p.

Berman, J. (2014). The History of Legal Theory and the Study of Biblical Law. CBQ, 76, 19–39.

Bickermann, B. (1967). Four Strange Books of the Bible, New York: Schocken.

Bills, N. (2020). A Theology of Justice in Exodus, Siphrut: Literature and Theology of the Hebrew Scriptures 26, University Park, PA: Eisenbrauns.

Bottéro, J. (1982). Le Code de Hammurabi. Annali della Scuola Normale Superiore di Pisa classe di lettere e filosophia, 12(3), 409–44.

Brueggemann, W. (1992). Old Testament Theology, P. Miller, ed., Minneapolis, MN: Fortress.

(1995). Pharaoh as Vassal. CBQ, 57, 27–51.

(1978). The Prophetic Imagination, Philadelphia, PA: Fortress.

(1985). A Shape for Old Testament Theology. CBQ, 47, 28–46.

Bucellati, G. (1995). Ethics and Piety in the Ancient Near East. In J. Sasson, ed., Civilizations of the Ancient Near East, 4 vols., Peabody, MA: Henrickson, pp. 3:1685–96.

Carmichael, C. (2000). The Three Laws on the Release of Slaves Ex 21, 2–11; Dtn 15, 12–18; Lev 25, 39–46. ZAW, 112, 509–25.

Cataldo, J. (2012). Breaking Monotheism: Yehud and the Material Formation of Monotheistic Identity, LHBOTS 565, London: Bloomsbury.

Chirichigno, G. (1993). Debt–Slavery in Israel and the Ancient Near East, JSOTSup 141, Sheffield: Sheffield Academic Press.

Ciholas, P. (1981). Monotheisme et violence. RSR, 69, 325–54.

Clements, R. (1980). Isaiah 1–39, NCBC, Grand Rapids, MI: Eerdmans.

Cobb, J. (1967). The Structure of Christian Existence, Philadelphia, PA: Westminster.

Comblin, J. (1985). Monotheism and Popular Religion, trans. D. Livingstone. In C. Geffré, J. P. Jossua, and M. Lefébure, eds., Monotheism, Concilium 177, Edinburgh: T & T Clark, pp. 91–9.

Craigie, P. (1976). The Book of Deuteronomy, NICOT, Grand Rapids, MI: Eerdmans.

Croatto, S. (1981). Exodus, trans. S. Attanasio, Maryknoll, NY: Orbis.

Davies, P. (1992). In Search of "Ancient Israel," JSOTSup 148, Sheffield: JSOT Press.

Dever, W. (2000). How Was Ancient Israel Different? In M. Lambert-Karlovsky, ed., The Breakout: The Origins of Civilization, Cambridge, MA: Harvard University Press, pp. 62–7.

Dietrich, W. (1994). Uber Werden und Wesen des biblischen Monotheismus. In W. Dietrich and M. Klopfenstein, eds., Ein Gott allein? JHWH-Verehrung und biblischer Monotheismus im Kontext der israelitischen und altorientalischen Religionsgeschichte, OBO 139, Göttingen: Vandenhoeck & Ruprecht, pp. 13–30.

Dietrich, W., and Klopfenstein, M., eds. (1994). Ein Gott allein? JHWH-Verehrung und biblischer Monotheismus im Kontext der israelitischen und altorientalischen Religionsgeschichte, OBO 139, Göttingen: Vandenhoeck & Ruprecht.

Driver, S. (1902). Deuteronomy, 3rd ed., ICC, Edinburgh: T & T Clark.

Dumas, A. (1985). The New Attraction of Neo-Paganism, trans. D. Smith. In C. Geffré, J. P. Jossua, and M. Lefébure, eds., Monotheism, Concilium 177, Edinburgh: T & T Clark, pp. 81–90.

Duquoc, C. (1985). Monotheism and Unitary Ideology, trans. R. Nowell. In C. Geffré, J. P. Jossua, and M. Lefébure, eds., Monotheism, Concilium 177, Edinburgh: T & T Clark, pp. 59–66.

Edelman, D., ed. (1996). The Triumph of Elohim, Grand Rapids, MI: Eerdmans.

Edwards, C. (1904). The Hammurabi Code and Sinaitic Legislation, Port Washington, NY: Kennikat.

Eichrodt, W. (1970). Ezekiel, trans. C. Quinn, OTL, Philadelphia, PA: Westminster.

Eisenstadt, S., ed. (1986). The Origins and Diversity of Axial Age Civilizations, Albany, NY: SUNY Press.

Elkana, Y. (1986). The Emergence of Second-order Thinking in Classical Greece. In S. Eisenstadt, ed., The Origins and Diversity of Axial Age Civilizations, SUNY Series in Near Eastern Studies, Albany, NY: SUNY Press, pp. 40–64.

Epsztein. (1986), Social Justice of the Ancient Near East and the People of the Bible, London: SCM Press.

Fager, J. (1987). Land Tenure in the Biblical Jubilee: A Moral World View. HAR, 11, 59–68.

Fensham, C. (1962). Widow, Orphan, and the Poor in Ancient Near Eastern Legal Literature. JNES, 21, 161–71.

Finkelstein, J. (1958). Bible and Babel: A Comparative Study of the Hebrew and Babylonian Religious Spirit. Commentary, 26, 431–44.

Fowden, G. (1993). Empire to Commonwealth, Princeton, NJ: Princeton University Press.

Frankl, G. (2005). The Three Faces of Monotheism: Judaism, Christianity, Islam, London: Open Gate Press.

Frick, F. (1985). The Formation of the State in Ancient Israel, SWBA 4, Sheffield: Almond.

Frymer-Kensky, T. (1992). In the Wake of the Goddesses, New York: Free Press.

Gamoran, H. (1971). The Biblical Law against Interest on Loans. JNES, 30, 127–34.

Garbini, G. (1988). History and Ideology in Ancient Israel, trans. J. Bowden, New York: Crossroad.

Garr, R. (2003). In His Own Image and Likeness: Humanity, Divinity, and Monotheism, CHANE 15, Leiden: Brill.

Geffré, C., Jossua, J. P., and Lefébure, M., eds. (1985). Monotheism, Concilium 177, Edinburgh,: T & T Clark.

Geller, S. (2000). The God of the Covenant. In B. Porter, ed., One God or Many? Concepts of Divinity in the Ancient World, Transactions of the Casio Bay Assyriological Institute 1, Portland, ME: TCBAI, pp. 273–319.

Gerstenberger, E. (2007). In der Schuldenfalle: Zwangsvollstreckung? Insolvenzregelungen in Lev 25 und ihre theologischen Folgen. BK, 62, 16–21.

(1996). Yahweh the Patriarch, trans. F. Gaiser, Minneapolis, MN: Fortress.

Gimbutas, M. (1974). The Gods and Goddesses of Old Europe, London: Thames & Hudson.

Gnuse, R. K. (2007). Breakthrough or Tyranny: Monotheism's Contested Implications. Hor, 34, 78–95.

(1999). The Emergence of Monotheism in Ancient Israel. Religion, 29, 315–36.

(1989). Heilsgeschichte as a Model for Biblical Theology, College Theology Society Studies in Religion 4, Lanham, MD: University Press of America.

(2021a). Human "Rule" over Nature in Genesis 1: A Better Understanding. International Journal of the Arts and the Humanities, 7(1), 64–71.

(1985). Jubilee Legislation in Leviticus. BTB, 15, 43–48.

(2021b). The "Living Soul" in People and Animals: Environmental Themes from Genesis 2. BTB, 51, 168–74.

(1994). New Directions in Biblical Theology. JAAR, 62, 893–918.

(1997). No Other Gods: Emergent Monotheism in Israel, JSOTSup 241, Sheffield.

(2011). No Tolerance for Tyrants: The Biblical Assault on Kings and Kingship, Collegeville, MN: Liturgical Press.

(2000). The Old Testament and Process Theology, St. Louis, MO: Chalice Press.

(2021c). Psalm 104: The Panorama of Life. BTB, 51, 4–14.

(2021d). Romans 1:16-17 Condemns the Isis Cult, not Homosexuality. International Journal of Research in Humanities and Social Sciences, 8(3), 33–41.

(2015a). Seven Gay Texts: Biblical Passages Used to Condemn Homosexuality. BTB, 45, 68–87.

(2015b). Trajectories of Justice: What the Bible Says about Slaves, Women, and Homosexuality, Eugene, OR: Wipf and Stock.

(1985). You Shall Not Steal: Community and Property in the Biblical Tradition, Maryknoll, NY: Orbis.

Goldenberg, R. (1998). The Nations That Know Thee Not, New York: New York University Press.

Greengus, S. (2000). Legal and Social Institutions of Ancient Mesopotamia. In J. Sasson, ed., Civilizations of the Ancient Near East, 4 vols., Peabody, MA: Hendrickson, pp. 1: 471–2.

Gross, R. (1999). Religious Diversity: Some Implications for Monotheism. Cross Currents, 49, 349–66.

Halpern, B. (1991). Jerusalem and the Lineages in the Seventh Century BCE: Kinship and the Rise of Individual Moral Liability. In B. Halpern and

D. Hobson, eds., Law and Ideology in Monarchic Israel, JSOTSup 124, Sheffield: JSOT Press, pp. 11–107.

Hamilton, J. (1992). Social Justice and Deuteronomy, SBLDS 136, Atlanta, GA: Scholars Press.

Hammershaimb, E. (1960). On the Ethics of the Old Testament Prophets. In Congress Volume (Oxford, 1959), VTSup 7, Leiden: Brill, pp. 75–101.

Handy, L. (1994). Among the Host of Heaven: The Syro-Palestinian Pantheon as Bureaucracy, Winona Lake, IN: Eisenbrauns.

Harper, W. R. (1904). Amos and Hosea, ICC, Edinburgh: T & T Clark.

Harris, R. (1995). The World of the Bible, London: Thames and Hudson.

Hayes, J. (1971). Introduction to the Bible, Philadelphia, PA: Westminster.

Hendel, R. (1992). Worldmaking in Ancient Israel. JSOT, 56, 3–18.

Hopkins, D. (1985). The Highlands of Canaan: Agricultural Life in the Early Iron Age, SWBA 3, Sheffield: Almond Press.

Houston, W. (2006). Contending for Justice: Ideologies and Theologies of Social Justice in the Old Testament, LHBOTS 428, London: T & T Clark.

Hudson, M. (1999). Proclaim Liberty throughout the Land: The Economic Roots of Jubilee. BibRev, 15(1), 26–33, 44.

Hyatt, J. (1971). Exodus, NCBC, London: Oliphants.

Jackson, B. S. (1989). Ideas of Law and Legal Administration. In R. Clements, ed., The World of Ancient Israel, Cambridge: Cambridge University Press, pp. 185–202.

Jaspers, K. (1953). The Origin and Goal of History, trans. M. Bullock, New Haven, CT: Yale University Press.

Kaiser, O. (1972). Isaiah 1–12, trans. R. A. Wilson, OTL, Philadelphia, PA: Westminster.

Käsemann, E. (1964). Ministry and Community in the New Testament. In Essays on New Testament Themes, trans. W. J. Montague, SBT 41, London: SCM Press, pp. 63–94.

Keel, O., ed. (1980). Monotheismus im Alten Israel und seiner Umwelt, BibB 14, Fribourg: Schweizerisches Katholisches Bibelwerk.

Kessler, R. (2010). Das Erlassjahrgesetz Dtn 15, 1–11. Ein Gebot und seine Umsetzung. TGl, 100, 15–30.

Kirsch, J. (2004). God against the Gods: The History of the War between Monotheism and Polytheism, New York: Viking Compass.

Knight, D. (2011). Law, Power, and Justice in Ancient Israel, Library of Ancient Israel, Louisville, KY: Westminster John Knox.

Lang, B. (1983). Monotheism and the Prophetic Minority, SWBA 1, Sheffield: Almond Press.

Lemaire, A. (2007). The Birth of Monotheism: The Rise and Disappearance of Yahwism, Washington, DC: BAS Press.

Lerner, G. (1986). The Creation of Patriarchy, New York: Oxford University Press.

Leuchter, M. (2008). The Manumission Laws in Leviticus and Deuteronomy: The Jeremiah Connection. JBL, 127, 635–53.

Loewenstamm, S. (1971). Law. In B. Mazar, ed., The Judges, WHJP 3, Newark, NJ: Rutgers University Press, pp. 231–67.

(1969). Neshek and m/tarbith. JBL, 88, 78–80.

Lohfink, N. (1983). Das Alte Testament und sein Monotheismus. In K. Rahner, ed., Der eine Gott und der dreieine Gott, Schriftenreihe der Katholischen Akademie der Erzdiözese Freiburg, Munich: Schnell und Steiner, pp. 28–47.

(1985). Zur Geschichte der Diskussion über den Monotheismus im Alten Israel. In H. Haag, ed., Gott, der Einzige. Zur Entstehung des Monotheismus im Israel, QD 104, Freiburg: Herder, pp. 9–25.

Lowery, R. (2000). Sabbath and Jubilee, St. Louis, MO: Chalice.

Luckert, K. (1991). Egyptian Light and Hebrew Fire, Albany, NY: SUNY.

Lutz, D. (1984). The Relative Influence of European Writers on Late Eighteenth Century American Political Thought. The American Political Science Review, 78, 189–97.

Malchow, B. (1966). Social Justice in the Hebrew Bible, Collegeville, MN: Liturgical Press.

Marquard, O. (1979). Lob des Polytheismus: über Monomythie und Polymythie. In H. Poser, ed., Philosophie und Mythos, Berlin: Walter de Gruyter, pp. 40–58.

Marshall, J. (1993). Israel and the Book of the Covenant, SBLDS 140, Atlanta, GA: Scholars Press.

Mays, J. L. (1969). Amos, OTL, Philadelphia, PA: Westminster.

(1976). Micah, OTL, Philadelphia, PA: Westminster.

Mendelsohn, I. (1949). Slavery in the Ancient Near East, New York: Oxford University Press.

Michaels, A. (1994). Monotheismus und Fundamentalismus. Eine These und ihre Gegenthese. In W. Dietrich and M. Klopfenstein, eds., Ein Gott allein? JHWH-Verehrung und biblischer Monotheismus im Kontext der israelitischen und altorientalischen Religionsgeschichte, OBO 139, Göttingen: Vandenhoeck & Ruprecht, pp. 51–7.

Milgrom, J. (1993). Sweet Land and Liberty. BibRev, 9(4), 8, 54.

Miller, P. (1985). Israelite Religion. In D. Knight and G. Tucker, eds., The Hebrew Bible and Its Modern Interpreters, Chico, CA: Scholars Press, pp. 201–37.

Mitchell, H. (1912). Ethics of the Old Testament, Chicago, IL: n.p.

Moltmann, J. (1985). The Inviting Unity of the Triune God, trans. R. Nowell. In C. Geffré, J. P. Jossua, and M. Lefébure, eds., Monotheism, Concilium 177, Edinburgh: T & T Clark, pp. 50–8.

de Moor, J. (1990). The Rise of Yahwism, BETL 91, Leuven: Leuven University/Peeters.

Morgenstern, J. (1962). Sabbatical Year. In G. Buttrick, ed., IDB, 4 vols., Nashville, TN: Abingdon, p. 4:142.

Moriarity, F. (1974). Word as Power in the Ancient Near East. In H. Bream, R. Heim, and C. Moore, eds., A Light unto My Path, Philadelphia, PA: Temple University Press, pp. 345–62.

Moyer, J. (1983). Hittite and Israelite Cultic Practices. In W. Hallo, J. Moyer, and L. Perdue, eds., Scripture in Context II, Winona Lake, IN: Eisenbrauns, pp. 19–38.

Nardoni, E. (2004). Rise Up, O Judge: A Study of Justice in the Biblical World, Peabody MA: Henderson.

Neufeld, E. (1955). The Prohibitions against Loans at Interest in Ancient Hebrew Law. HUCA, 226, 359–62, 375–410.

Nicholson, E. (1991). Deuteronomy's Vision of Israel. In D. Garrone and F. Israele, eds. Storia e tradizione di Israel, Brescia: Paideia Editrice, pp. 191–204.

Niehr, H. (1990). Der höchste Gott, BZAW 190, Berlin: Walter de Gruyter.

Nikiprowetsky, V. (1975). Ethical Monotheism. Daedalus, 104(2), 68–89.

North, R. (1954). Sociology of the Biblical Jubilee, AnBib 4, Rome: Pontifical Biblical Institute.

Oswalt, J. (1986). The Book of Isaiah 1–39, NICOT, Grand Rapids, MI: Eerdmans.

Otto, E. (1994). Theologische Ethik des Alten Testaments, Theologische Wissenschaft 3,(2), Stuttgart: Kohlhammer.

Pakkala, J. (2009). The Date of the Oldest Edition of Deuteronomy. ZAW, 121, 388–419.

  (2010). Why the Cult Reforms in Judah Probably Did Not Happen. In R. Kratz and H. Spieckermann, eds., One God – One Cult – One Nation: Archaeological and Biblical Perspectives, BZAW 45, Berlin: Walter de Gruyter, pp. 201–35.

Petersen, D. (1988). Israel and Monotheism: The Unfinished Agenda. In G. Tucker, D. Petersen, and R. Wilson, eds., Canon, Theology, and Old Testament Interpretation, Philadelphia, PA: Fortress, pp. 92–107.

Pfeiffer, H. (2015). Jahwes Kommen von Süden: Jdc 5; Hab 3; Dtr 33 und Ps 68 in ihrem literatur- und theologiegeschichtlichen Umfeld, FRLANT 211, Göttingen : Vandenhoeck & Ruprecht.

(2017). The Origin of Yhwh and Its Attestations. In J. van Oorschot and M. Witte, eds., The Origins of Yahwism, BZAW 484, Berlin: Walter de Gruyter, pp. 115–44.

Phillips, A. (1970). Ancient Israel's Criminal Law: A New Approach to The Decalogue, Oxford: Blackwell.

(1973). Deuteronomy, CBC, Cambridge: Cambridge University Press.

Porter, J. R. (1976). Leviticus, CBC, Cambridge: Cambridge University Press.

(1979). Old Testament Historiography. In G. Anderson, ed., Tradition and Interpretation, Oxford: Clarendon, pp. 125–62.

Pleins, D. (2001). The Social Visions of the Hebrew Bible, Louisville, KY: Westminster John Knox.

Pruitt, B. (2010). The Sabbath Year of Release: The Social Location and Practice of Semittah in Deuteronomy 15:1–18. Restoration Quarterly, 52, 81–92.

Roth, M., ed. (1997). Law Collections from Mesopotamia and Asia Minor, 2nd ed. SBLWAW 6, Atlanta, GA: Scholars Press.

Saggs, H. W. F. (1995). Babylonians, Norman, OK: University of Oklahoma Press.

(1978). The Encounter with the Divine in Mesopotamia and Israel, London: Athlone.

Schwartz, R. (1997). The Curse of Cain, Chicago, IL: University of Chicago Press.

Smith, M. (1990). The Early History of God, San Francisco, CA: Harper and Row.

(2001). The Origins of Biblical Monotheism, New York: Oxford University Press.

Smith, M., and Hoffman, J. (1989). What the Bible Really Says, San Francisco, CA: HarperCollins.

Snaith, N. (1967). Leviticus and Numbers, Century Bible, New York: Nelson.

Sperling, D. (1986). Israel's Religion in the Ancient near East. In A. Green, ed., Jewish Spirituality, World Spirituality: An Encyclopedic History of the Religious Quest 13, New York: Crossroad, pp. 5–31.

Stackert, J. (2011). The Sabbath of the Land in the Holiness Legislation: Combining Priestly and Non-Priestly Perspectives. CBQ, 73, 239–50.

Stark, R. (2013). For the Glory of God: How Monotheism Led to Reformations, Science Witch-Hunts, and the End of Slavery, Princeton, NJ: Princeton University Press.

(2001). One True God: Historical Consequences of Monotheism, Princeton, NJ: Princeton University Press.

Stein, S. (1953). The Laws on Interest in the Old Testament. JTS, 4, 161–70.

Stolz, F. (1994). Der Monotheismus Israels im Kontext der altorientalischen Religionsgeschichte–Tendenzen neuerer Forschung. In W. Dietrich and M. Klopfenstein, eds., Ein Gott allein? JHWH-Verehrung und biblischer Monotheismus im Kontext der israelitischen und altorientalischen Religionsgeschichte, OBO 139, Göttingen: Vandenhoeck & Ruprecht, pp. 33–50.

Theissen, G. (1985). Biblical Faith: An Evolutionary Approach, trans. J. Bowden. Philadelphia, PA: Fortress.

Tremmel, W. (1984). Religion, What Is It?, 2nd ed., New York: Holt, Rinehart & Winston.

Uffenheimer, B. (1986). Myth and Reality in Ancient Israel. In S. Eisenstadt, ed., The Origins and Diversity of Axial Age Civilizations, SUNY Series in Near Eastern Studies, Albany: SUNY Press, pp. 135–68.

Van Seters, J. (2003). A Law Book for the Diaspora: Revision in the Study of the Covenant Code, New York: Oxford University Press.

Varso, M. (2008). Interest (Usury) and Its Variations in the Biblical Law Codices. Communio Viatorum, 50, 323–38.

De Vaux, R. (1961). Ancient Israel: Its Life and Institutions, trans. J. McHugh, New York: McGraw Hill.

Veyne, P. (1987). The Roman Empire. In P. Veyne, ed., A History of the Private Life, I From Pagan Rome to Byzantium, trans. A. Goldhammer, Cambridge, MA: Belknap.

Wacholder, B. Z. (1973). The Calendar of Sabbatical Cycles during the Second Temple and Early Rabbinic Period. HUCA, 44, 158–84.

(1976). Sabbatical Year. In K. Crim, ed., IDBSup, Nashville, TN: Abingdon, pp. 762–3.

Watson, A. (1985). The Evolution of Law, Oxford: Blackwell.

Weavers, J. (1969). Ezekiel, NCBC, Grand Rapids, MI: Eerdmans.

Weber, M. (1952). Ancient Judaism, trans. H. Gerth and D. Martindale, Glencoe, IL: Free Press.

Wright, C. (1996). Deuteronomy, NIBC, Peabody, MA: Henrickson.

Zenger, E. (2003). Der Monotheismus Israel: Entstehung – Profil – Relevanz. In T. Söding, ed., Ist Der Glaube Feind der Freiheit? Die Neue Debatte um den Monotheismus, QD 196, Freiburg: Herder, pp. 9–52.

Cambridge Elements ≡

Religion and Monotheism

Paul K. Moser
Loyola University Chicago
Paul K. Moser is Professor of Philosophy at Loyola University Chicago. He is the author of *Paul's Gospel of Divine Self-Sacrifice; The Divine Goodness of Jesus; Divine Guidance; Understanding Religious Experience; The God Relationship; The Elusive God* (winner of national book award from the Jesuit Honor Society); *The Evidence for God; The Severity of God; Knowledge and Evidence* (all Cambridge University Press); and *Philosophy after Objectivity* (Oxford University Press); co-author of *Theory of Knowledge* (Oxford University Press); editor of *Jesus and Philosophy* (Cambridge University Press) and *The Oxford Handbook of Epistemology* (Oxford University Press); co-editor of *The Wisdom of the Christian Faith* (Cambridge University Press). He is the co-editor with Chad Meister of the book series *Cambridge Studies in Religion, Philosophy, and Society.*

Chad Meister
Affiliate Scholar, Ansari Institute for Global Engagement with Religion, University of Notre Dame
Chad Meister is Affiliate Scholar at the Ansari Institute for Global Engagement with Religion at the University of Notre Dame. His authored and co-authored books include *Evil: A Guide for the Perplexed* (Bloomsbury Academic, 2nd edition); *Introducing Philosophy of Religion* (Routledge); *Introducing Christian Thought* (Routledge, 2nd edition); and *Contemporary Philosophical Theology* (Routledge). He has edited or co-edited the following: *The Oxford Handbook of Religious Diversity* (Oxford University Press); *Debating Christian Theism* (Oxford University Press); with Paul Moser, *The Cambridge Companion to the Problem of Evil* (Cambridge University Press); and with Charles Taliaferro, *The History of Evil* (Routledge, in six volumes). He is the co-editor with Paul Moser of the book series *Cambridge Studies in Religion, Philosophy, and Society.*

About the Series
This Cambridge Element series publishes original concise volumes on monotheism and its significance. Monotheism has occupied inquirers since the time of the Biblical patriarch, and it continues to attract interdisciplinary academic work today. Engaging, current, and concise, the Elements benefit teachers, researched, and advanced students in religious studies, Biblical studies, theology, philosophy of religion, and related fields.

Cambridge Elements ⁼

Religion and Monotheism

Elements in the Series

A full series listing is available at: www.cambridge.org/er&m

Printed in the United States
by Baker & Taylor Publisher Services